TESTIMONIALS

"Jason's a great fit for folks who live for that extra bit of pizzaz that can elevate otherwise ordinary moments to something much more unique and fun. By sheer luck I've had the pleasure of attending FOUR of Jason's weddings . . . One more and I get a free wedding!"

– Darren Criss

"Our day was zero percent stress and a hundred percent joy. Jason made that possible. He gets our highest recommendation."

– Steve Pasquale & Phillipa Soo

"Working with Jason was like having a best friend who also happens to be a world-class producer. He understood our vision completely and elevated every detail, making our wedding day unforgettable. He handled every twist and turn of our intricate wedding with incredible professionalism and heart. His ability to balance logistics with emotional intelligence made all the difference, and we truly couldn't have done it without him."

– Garrett Clayton & Blake Knight

"New York weddings can be daunting—especially in our case, inviting a bunch of actors on a Monday (which could've been like herding cats). But JMK was unstoppable, handling every detail with grace, humor, and effortless style. He took our chaos and turned it into pure magic. He understood we wanted the classic elegance of a New York wedding without the fuss. At every turn, he had suggestions to keep a touch of whimsy to the chic downtown New York proceedings so that our guests (and us!) could truly relax and enjoy the night."

– Erika Henningsen & Kyle Selig

"Jason knows everything one could possibly know about planning a wedding. On top of that he happens to be a wonderfully entertaining writer as well. Get this book then go out there and get married!"

– Augustus Prew & Jeffery Self

"For our wedding, we wanted something personal, full of heart, music, humor, and meaningful touches that felt unmistakably us—and Jason not only listened, he truly got us. He collaborated with us every step of the way, bringing our vision to life with care, creativity, and the comforting presence of someone who felt like (and has become!) a lifelong friend."

– Drew Gehling & Julia Mattison

"Jason was an incredible person to work with. Easy going, understood all our quirk and whimsy, and executed it flawlessly. He went above and beyond—even finagled Bernadette Peters to leave us a congratulatory voice message. He played it just as we cut into our Bernadette Peters Rice Krispie Treat Wedding cake. Did we mention it was quirky?"

– Gideon Glick

"Working with Jason is like planning a wedding with one of your best friends ... one of your best friends who also happens to know absolutely everything about planning weddings. A fabulous experience. 10/10 would recommend."

– Alysha Umphress

We Do

An Inclusive Guide When a Traditional Wedding Won't Cut It

JASON MITCHELL KAHN

Copyright © 2025 Jason Mitchell Kahn. All rights reserved.

No part of this publication shall be reproduced, transmitted, or sold in whole or in part in any form without prior written consent of the author, except as provided by the United States of America copyright law. Any unauthorized usage of the text without express written permission of the publisher is a violation of the author's copyright and is illegal and punishable by law. All trademarks and registered trademarks appearing in this guide are the property of their respective owners.

For permission requests, write to the publisher, addressed "Attention: Permissions Coordinator," at the address below.

Publish Your Purpose
141 Weston Street, #155
Hartford, CT, 06141

The opinions expressed by the Author are not necessarily those held by Publish Your Purpose.

Ordering Information: Quantity sales and special discounts are available on quantity purchases by corporations, associations, and others. For details, contact the author at WeDo@JMKandCO.com.

Edited by: Nancy Graham-Tillman and Emily Ribeiro
Cover design by: Nelly Murariu
Typeset by: Medlar Publishing Solutions Pvt Ltd., India

Printed in the United States of America.

ISBN: 979-8-88797-144-5 (hardcover)
ISBN: 979-8-88797-145-2 (paperback)
ISBN: 979-8-88797-146-9 (ebook)

Library of Congress Control Number: 2025902032

First edition, September 2025.

The information contained within this book is strictly for informational purposes. The material may include information, products, or services by third parties. As such, the Author and Publisher do not assume responsibility or liability for any third-party material or opinions. The publisher is not responsible for websites (or their content) that are not owned by the publisher. Readers are advised to do their own due diligence when it comes to making decisions.

Publish Your Purpose is a hybrid publisher of non-fiction books. Our mission is to elevate the voices often excluded from traditional publishing. We intentionally seek out authors and storytellers with diverse backgrounds, life experiences, and unique perspectives to publish books that will make an impact in the world. Do you have a book idea you would like us to consider publishing? Please visit PublishYourPurpose.com for more information.

CONTENTS

	MY AUDITION	xi
	My I Dos	xii
	Who Am I Anyway?	xvi
	Endnotes	xxvi
1	WRITING YOUR SCRIPT	1
	Dreaming	2
	Organizing	16
2	THE PRODUCERS MEETING	25
	Target Budget	26
	Actual Budget	27
	Guest List	37
	Endnote	45
3	BOOKING THE THEATER	47
	Place	50
	Time	59
4	THE DIRECTOR'S TOUCH	77
	The Cast List	78
	The Script	84

5 ADVERTISING YOUR SHOW ... 109
- Save the Dates ... 111
- Invitations ... 115
- Supporting Elements ... 123
- Other Printed Materials ... 127

6 DOCUMENTING YOUR WORK ... 139
- Photography ... 139
- Videography ... 144
- Content Creation ... 146
- From Stage to Screen ... 147

7 COMPOSING THE SCORE ... 155
- Bands ... 156
- DJs ... 159
- Finding Harmony ... 160
- Other Options ... 162
- The Orchestration ... 162
- Other Entertainment ... 171

8 THE CONCESSIONS ... 177
- Food ... 177
- Settling on the Menu ... 183
- The Cake ... 186
- Sugar, Butter, Flour ... 189
- Late-Night Bites ... 189
- Beverages ... 190
- Endnote ... 198

9 SET DESIGN ... 201
- The Pros ... 202
- Scene-by-Scene Layout ... 205
- Furniture ... 210
- Flooring ... 215
- Lighting ... 216

CONTENTS

10 SET DECORATION & ACTIVATIONS 223
    Flowers 223
    Candles 229
    Linens 230
    Draping 231
    Tabletops 232
    Activations 233

11 COSTUME DESIGN 243
    Style 244
    Silhouettes & Necklines 246
    Fabrics, Colors & Finishes 252
    Trains 252
    Veils 253
    Suits & Tuxes 254
    Accessories 259
    Group Looks 266
    Let's Get Physical 267
    I Feel Pretty 268

12 OPENING NIGHT 275
    Final Numbers & Seating 276
    Accommodations & Welcome Bags 277
    Transportation 279
    Parking 280
    Weather 280
    Gifts 281
    Final Payments & Gratuities 281
    Honeymoon 282
    Pack-Up 283
    Run of Show 283
    Curtain Up 288

CURTAIN CALL	.291
APPENDIX: EXPERT INSIGHTS	.293
ACKNOWLEDGMENTS	.299
ABOUT THE AUTHOR	.303

MY AUDITION

I'd like to propose a toast. I believe congratulations are in order. Even though I know we should never assume, I can only guess you

- just got engaged (congrats!),
- are thinking about popping the question (I applaud you for starting your research in advance),
- have been engaged for a while and are finally ready to have a wedding (you've come to the right place), or
- do not fall into any of the above categories but just want to support me (I thank you from the bottom of my heart, and thanks Mom).

If you fall anywhere along the spectrum of those options, you've taken an important first step. Perhaps you've already peered into the wedding industry. I mean, if you've ever typed the word "wedding" into your search browser, chances are the algorithm is now showing you all sorts of products you didn't know existed or aren't ready to face. Have any of these thoughts already raced through your head?

- I don't even know where to begin.
- I'm a man who hasn't spent my life dreaming of what my wedding will look like.
- I'm a woman who doesn't seem to have the "bride gene."
- I don't identify by sex or gender and don't see myself in a wedding.
- We're a throuple; how wide should the aisle be?

If so, this book is for you.

MY I DOs

When I first pitched the idea of writing this book, one of the subtitles I considered was "An Inclusive Guide for Anyone Who Has Felt Othered While Planning Their Wedding." In my career, I've planned hundreds of weddings, and those are the types of couples I've always connected with the most. As a professional wedding planner, I've always espoused working with those who don't identify with titles, not only brides and grooms. I wrote my first guide, *Getting Groomed: The Ultimate Wedding Planner for Gay Grooms*, over a decade ago; I'm still proud of it, but a lot has changed since then. We've lived through a global pandemic, a gut-punching reality show of a political roller coaster, and the evolution of our language around sex, gender, and pronouns. Technology also continues to develop faster than Taylor Swift sells out an arena. I just read an article about a couple who used AI to plan their entire wedding . . . and then I needed a martini with a best friend to assure me I had a future.

The point is, we live in an ever-changing world. And in terms of weddings, a lot has changed. As a gay adolescent, I never dreamed I'd grow up in a world where people like me got married regularly, let alone that planning such weddings would become my career. However, there are some elements about weddings that really haven't changed and some tried and true basic facts that have stood the test of time for a reason. We'll get into all of that in this book. What's most important is that you've beaten the odds, found a special

MY AUDITION

partner, and are ready to formally declare that love before family and friends—and any exes you want to impress.

Whether marriage is right for the two of you is quite possibly the most important decision you need to make, preferably before you're financially committed to any of the fabulous wedding trends of the year. As I say to all Jason Mitchell Kahn (JMK) couples, there's a huge difference between planning a wedding and living in a marriage. I feel I'm an expert at helping you with the first one. As for the latter, marriage is a serious commitment and carries a great deal of weight emotionally, politically, and spiritually. If you're unsure whether marriage is right for the two of you, this is not the book to address that issue. If, however, you're looking to understand everything that can go into a wedding and then decide from that list what you'd like to incorporate into yours, and if, hopefully, you find my sense of humor entertaining along the way, then this is the book for you.

I firmly believe that no two weddings should look or feel the same and that each event should uniquely represent the couple it's for. There's a process to achieving that, and that's what this book lays out for you. It's also filled with tips, because sometimes just the tip is all you need. I'll also share some tricks, because sometimes just a new trick can open your eyes and make you feel something sudden and new. And if those past two sentences took you elsewhere, then snap out of it! We're talking wedding planning here, which I firmly believe is more enjoyable when we can do it with a sense of humor. You'll also notice several theatrical references throughout the book. Before I worked in the world of weddings, I came from theater. Having worked in both industries and been labeled "Broadway's Wedding Planner" by *Playbill*, I can attest there are many similarities between theater and the process of creating weddings. There are also many key differences, but the path to opening night is similar.

I caution you now that reading this book may have some different effects on you:

- It might make you feel organized, relaxed, and excited to pull off the event of your dreams.

- It might make you realize what a huge undertaking planning a wedding can be and that you need a professional to do this for you. If this is you, don't be shy in reaching out! Maybe you're the next JMK couple, or I can recommend one of my thousands of colleagues around the world.
- You might discover that even with me guiding the way, you still have a ton of decisions to make.
- It might make you question other people's choices when it comes to weddings.
- You might realize having a wedding isn't actually what you want.

If the last option is your path, have a fabulous elopement. For everything else, there's Mastercard—and me. I'll be here to remind you to stop, breathe, and relax. We're planning an event that's meant to literally spark joy. This book will guide you through all the neutral tasks (selecting a delicious menu is a necessity for all weddings) as well as the aspects of wedding planning that might be a little confusing if you feel othered, such as deciding how you might word your invitations. I'm here to tell you that you *can* have a fabulous event without all the unnecessary stress typically associated with planning a wedding.

Whether one of you popped the question on a billboard in Times Square or you mutually agreed over delicious takeout, you're now officially engaged and it's time to celebrate on your terms. After one of my friends surprised their partner with a proposal, the partner felt it was only fair to plan a surprise counter proposal so they both could experience the excitement of being proposed to. Anything goes, really. But before we get into bow ties and boutonnieres, it's important to know that several couples have confessed that being engaged was one of the best times of their lives, so take some time to enjoy this newfound status.

Have you already "put a ring on it" to make it official? I ask not to remind you of the second *Sex and the City* film (I mean, I'm not a monster) but because it's important for you to know that

MY AUDITION

just like your wedding, your engagement does not have to be traditional. The beauty is in the question, answer, and sincerity, not in the object that accompanies it. Rings are certainly the tradition for making an engagement official, but it's okay if neither of you took on the daunting task of picking out a ring to surprise the other. There are many other options I'll tell you about in the first chapter.

As we embark on this journey together, even though you're the ones who'll be exchanging vows, I must say some I DOs upfront:

- ☑ I DO promise to help you organize and define the choices that work for you, answer all your questions, and guide you through a process that should be fun, not frenzied.
- ☑ I DO promise to keep this book as concise as possible so that I don't overwhelm you. If you have a question not covered here, feel free to reach out.
- ☑ I DO promise to keep you focused and calm. The byline of my company is "Keep Calm and Marry On" for a reason! Couples often spend their engagements pleasing outside parties, such as parents, in-laws, and family expectations. That's not the JMK way! This event must be on *your* terms.
- ☑ I DO promise to constantly ask you questions to which your answers will create the roadmap of an event that feels personal, bespoke, and reflective of the two of you.
- ☑ I DO promise to remind you that words such as "standard," "typical," "expected," and "traditional" are not required for the choices you make.
- ☑ I DO promise to remind you that outside opinions aren't always the best. I've spent hours of my career stopping clients from spiraling after they opened certain planning decisions to friends and family.

Throughout my career, I've been fortunate enough to get a decent amount of press, and there are two questions that seem to recur during interviews. The first is, "What is a signature Jason

Mitchell Kahn wedding?" While I've been known for pulling off huge surprises, designing automated chuppahs, and hiring many drag queens, the answer always remains the same: It's not about me. Weddings are reflections of the couples and therefore look and feel very different from one to the next.

The other question I've frequently been asked since I started in the business is, "What is the biggest difference between a gay and a straight wedding?" I used to always correct people by saying we refer to them as "same-sex" and "opposite-sex weddings," respectively, but I've learned we're even moving away from those labels now. But I digress.

What I've observed in steadily planning all kinds of weddings for quite some time now is this: Heteronormative culture has taught us that a wedding is "the bride's day." And with many of the couples I've worked with who identify as heterosexual, the groom is usually much less involved, if even at all. Some grooms I never meet for the first time until their weddings! I've still had wonderful experiences and am very proud of those weddings, but the process has been different with queer or nontraditional couples. I've found they approach planning the wedding together with equal footing; it's *their* day. And in my vast experience of creating these events, I can attest that three heads are better than two.

Are you ready for the three of us to dive in and dream, create, and execute a wedding that's exclusively yours? If your answer is also the title of this book, then join me on a first date and keep reading. If you'd rather get to work and skip getting to know me, proceed to chapter 1 (just don't tell me you did).

WHO AM I ANYWAY?

Since we've just begun our newfound throuple—and yes that's what my clients tell me it's like working together—I wanted to give you a bit more background into who I am. As I look back, so much of my life experiences have shaped how I plan weddings, including how I view them as opportunities to tell a couple's love story. As a wedding planner, I allow all my clients to get very personal with me, so that's what I want to do with you.

So how did I become the sequined-tuxedo-wearing Jason Mitchell Kahn? Contrary to popular belief, I did not go to college and major in gay weddings. But I have had so many moments in my career when my inner narrator has said, "Pinch me now! Is this really happening?" Once, I was on my knees offering a corsage to Mariah Carey at her nephew's wedding that I'd planned, and she said, "Tie it on me, baby." Later I was escorting her to her seat, and she looked at me and said, "Boy, you're stricter than the Grammy's." As she was leaving that night, she came to say goodbye, and after I smiled and thanked her for coming, she said, "You're a star!" At another wedding, I found myself changing out of my load-in clothes and into my tux in a coat check closet with Kelli O'Hara, who was practicing a surprise performance for the couple. She looked at me when she finished and said, "What did you think?" to which I said, "I can't give you notes." And when I wrote my first book, the iconic Joan Rivers agreed to provide a quote for the front cover and in the process told me she considered me to be a good friend! She also once stated something revolutionary that holds very tried and true: "Any straight person complaining about the Supreme Court striking down DOMA should be forced to hire a heterosexual wedding planner."[1] I have so many other stories I could share, and they all point to two key concepts: (1) I always have and always will love a true diva, and (2) when I look back at the life experiences that led me here, I see that in many ways the universe did provide me with a hands-on education along the way.

I have identified as gay for quite some time. I came out of the closet at age seventeen, and a few years later my sister, my one and only sibling, came out as lesbian. The first wedding I ever planned was for her and her wife, and six years later when they wanted to begin a family, they asked me to be the donor; and together we created two children that my sister-in-law carried. It would be an understatement to say we're a very queer family. We have loving and accepting liberal parents who are so proud to have two gay children and support us at every endeavor in life. I'm also lucky enough to have a robust circle of friends who all identify differently. Some are gay, some are lesbian, some are nonbinary, some are gender fluid or gender neutral, some are pansexual, and some are trans. And yes, I'm also friends with some people who identify as straight. I personally identify 100 percent gay, and my pronouns are he/him/tuxedo.

My sister and I have enjoyed the incredible experience of identifying as gay siblings for over twenty years now. But it didn't start that way, and both our individual and collective journeys really shaped me. From the time she was very young, my sister was the epitome of well-liked and cool. She excelled at everything from academics and sports to popularity. I was the exact opposite. I was painfully awkward and never knew how to fit in. As a young boy, I felt that my whole existence was defined by how I did in sports, but I was unathletic, uncoordinated, and uninterested. I was also always the shortest kid in class, so I was an easy target for bullying. And I was bullied. All the time. But eventually I found an escape: the theater. I was fortunate enough to have a mother who was, and still is, a professional theater director. I remember in first grade bringing one of her scripts to show and tell and explaining to my class what blocking was. On the weekends I'd ask my mom, "Is there any way that instead of trying to play with the other boys in the neighborhood I could go with you to help paint sets or make costumes?" I can now identify this as just wanting to be in a place where I felt safe. So I fell in love with the magic of live theater early on, and it never left me. By the time I was a young teenager, I decided there was nothing else I could ever do in life but be in theater, so I committed wholeheartedly.

Now, as an adult living in New York, going to the theater is still one of my favorite things to do. When I arrive, I turn off my phone, not only to be a responsible patron and avoid the wrath of Patti LuPone, but because I want to disconnect. The house lights dim, and I'm transported somewhere else, somewhere that's happening live and in real time, and I'm sharing the experience only with the people who've chosen to be in the audience that night. In an advertisement for AMC Theatres, poet laureate Nicole Kidman says it best: "Heartbreak feels good in a place like this."[2] Eventually, I learned that this one-night-only sensation I loved could be recreated with weddings.

    Where did I first discover what an epic love story could be? I grew up always hearing the story of my Grandma Edna and Grandpa Vic. My family is Jewish, and both of them came from families in Eastern Europe who immigrated to America before World War II. In fact, at age eighteen my grandfather very proudly enrolled in the American army to fight against the Nazis, and he met my grandmother at a USO dance during the war. For him, it was love at first sight, and for her she thought they'd never see each other again. After they met, he went back overseas and began writing to her. He aimed for a love letter a day and often said finding the time to write to her was the only thing that gave him hope during the darkness of war. This went on for over two years. In one exchange, Grandma Edna sent him a care package overseas. She knew Grandpa Vic missed familiar Jewish things, so she included a mezuzah necklace that he wore until the day he died, and, almost as a joke, a can of gefilte fish. He received the package on a Thursday, and being a religious man he opted to save it for Shabbat, putting the can in his backpack. Later that day, he was in a battle where he felt the sensation of a gunshot. Afterward, he opened his bag and found a bullet lodged in the can of gefilte fish, which had saved his life. He knew it was a sign that if he survived, he would marry this woman. His final station was in Japan, where he spent all the money he had on white silk and shipped it to my grandmother, writing, "If I come home alive, you will turn this into a dress." That did happen, and they married and had four children, the first being my mother. By the way, the two years of letters were saved, and all of us in the family were able to read the exchanges of the teenagers who created our family. It was a pretty epic love story.

    In our religion, as we approach the age of thirteen, we have a bar or bat mitzvah. How they're done now has changed a bit from when I was that age, but in the nineties and in the community I grew up in they were big productions that had themes. My mother hired what was known as a local "party planner," and I was fascinated with everything she did. While theater was my biggest love, "Jasonway" instead of Broadway didn't have enough of a ring to it, so we landed on "Jasonwood" and decided it would be like a Hollywood premier. There was a red carpet where guests entered, and huge posters of iconic films such as *Gone with the Wind* all read, "Starring Jason." For the backdrop behind the band, we designed a replica of the Hollywood hills with the iconic sign that would read "Jasonwood." As this was the nineties, my main color was teal green, the same color as the foamcore hills.

That morning, I had my service at a temple where I "began the journey of becoming a man," which is quite rich since I was about four feet ten, years away from my voice dropping, and already obsessed with Bette Midler. My family and I went home and rested before I changed into my ill-fitting rental tuxedo with a bright multi-colored vest, then we drove to the reception venue early for photos. What did I discover when I walked into the final stages of an event set up for a thirteen-year-old boy? Our party planner had measured for the foam hills from the floor to the ceiling, not accounting for the fact that the band would be on a stage. There was no way to trim the hills down on-site. As the party planner explained this to my mother, I had a meltdown. I remember saying to my mother, "How did she not know there would be a stage? How can we have Jasonwood without the hills?" I was sobbing as I watched the planner's team remove the letters from the hills and turn them into a new staggered pattern that would float on the black drape behind the band. One of the most valuable lessons about events that I espouse today came from my mother in that moment: She calmed me down and reminded me the most important thing was that all the family and friends would still be there to love, support, and celebrate me no matter what. I also learned that night that a saying I heard all the time in theater could also be true at these occasions: "The show must go on." In many ways, perhaps the night of my bar mitzvah is when the event planner was born. And for the record, a

MY AUDITION

JMK event would never forget to account for both a set *and* a stage, thank you very much.

Besides my bar mitzvah, that year contained some other important events with my parents. They took me to my first Bette Midler concert, which solidified her place in my life as the most fabulous diva around. We also went to see one of the biggest movies of the year, *Philadelphia*. As I got into high school and remained a die-hard thespian, I learned something vital: Being in the theater department was fun not only because we were constantly putting on productions but also because it's where I met other boys who were curious to try kissing while show tunes played on CDs. There was a duality, though, that started to exist as I began to understand why I had felt so different growing up. Discovering I found men attractive was both thrilling and completely terrifying. The only thing I understood at the time about gay men was that they all died from AIDS. That was all I knew about the few gay men who were somehow in my life and from the stories I heard. By the time I was a senior, I had my first boyfriend and truly felt comfortable in my own skin. I was gay, and I couldn't wait to spread the word. I was determined to do whatever possible to avoid getting sick, and I felt so complete and comfortable. My parents had been expecting this for years, so after I finally told them, I later lamented, "That was the most undramatic coming-out conversation ever!"

Because I felt like myself in theater and still believed there was nothing else I could ever do, I went to college to really train in it. Several of the plays we studied were about the AIDS crisis, and as a freshman I had one of those moments in life when in one instant everything changed: I discovered the play *Bent*. If you're unfamiliar with it, it tells the story of gay men who were persecuted by the Nazis during World War II. I was so shocked. As someone raised Jewish, and as someone who felt I knew a lot about what happened during that time, I was dumbfounded that not only were there gay victims, but there was a flourishing gay community in existence before the Nazis destroyed it. In the early 1930s, there were more than one hundred gay clubs and bars in Berlin,[3] and it's estimated that when the Nazis Party took power in 1933, they marked over one hundred thousand men with a pink triangle on their uniforms and placed them in camps.[4] My heart broke then, and still does now, thinking of all the potential art, music, poetry, culture, and love these innocent people could've created. I became obsessed. How did I not know about the people who should've been my chosen family? As I learned, the main reason is that so few of them lived to tell their stories. And in 1945 when the war ended, those who did survive were hardly welcomed into society; in fact, at least some version of the law that had allowed them to be arrested, called Paragraph 175, remained in effect until 1969.[5] Time and time again, I talked to other gay people about these facts and they had no idea. We don't come out and find ourselves in a class on gay history. I have always felt the obligation to honor these victims, including my chosen gay grandparents, and try to tell their stories.

After graduating from college, I moved to New York City. Besides being the theater capital of America, Manhattan always had a glamorous and fast-paced lifestyle associated with it that I'd never lived but was enamored by. I had no real plans, but I got an apartment, some black-and-white headshots, and a job waiting tables. I had no experience, but I knew I could play the role of someone knowledgeable about food, wine, and the city. I started with lunch shifts, made tons of mistakes, and was yelled at and made to feel less than every day. I eventually got the hang of it, though, and waiting tables turned out to be one of the greatest lessons in learning how to multitask, read people for where they are, and understand timing of service.

While learning the meaning of "mise en place" and the five varietals that make a Bordeaux blend, I realized I didn't want to be a professional actor but instead focus on my playwriting. The first play I wrote was *The Red Box*, a piece of historical fiction about the subject I was most passionate about. Two teenage boys meet in Germany in the 1930s. One marries a woman to hide, and the other is captured and put into a camp for being both gay and Jewish. It premiered in New York when I was twenty-five years old. Over the next few years, I wrote another play, *The Boys Upstairs*. That one was

MY AUDITION

based on the life I was living, a comedy about sex and dating in the city and celebrating all the incredible gay friendships I'd encountered. I can still feel the rush of those opening nights, and I later realized it's why I love being on-site for all the weddings I plan.

In between plays, when I made no money, I changed jobs to a new location. I became a server at the infamous Soho House New York. While it's now a global brand, there were only a few in London when I started, and they had just opened the first one in America. It was a company that didn't care about resumes and believed in promoting from within. Quickly they wanted me to grow from being a server to a manager, but I wasn't interested in running their restaurant or bar. But when they offered me a position in their events department, I soon went from being an events captain to a manager. Given the nature of Soho House, I was given the most incredible hands-on opportunity to learn about events by doing. I worked on birthday parties, gala dinners, fashion shows, movie premiers, book launches, holiday parties, and weddings.

I have to say, working there I got to do some really cool things, including a private party for Beyoncé and Madonna and a talent dinner for the late Betty White. And I was respected because of my competence at running events. But I never truly loved it or saw myself doing it for years. When I worked on a wedding for one of our members, something felt different. I wasn't able to articulate it immediately, but eventually I put it together. As a playwright, all I ever wanted to do was tell stories that were meaningful to people. Weddings, at least the way I see them, are stories to be told. I've met tons of other planners who prefer corporate events because they don't like the emotional stakes of weddings. For me, that's why I do it. No matter the scale of a wedding, I know the significance for the couple. At the time, it's usually the most important day of their lives, and I get to play a role in it! I don't think there's anything more gratifying.

As I was processing and putting all this together in my professional life, we had some exciting political achievements in America, including the legalization of same-sex marriage. First it went state by state, and New York was the fourth state to do this. Everyone in the event industry was buzzing about how many new opportunities same-sex weddings would bring. I'd also just gotten engaged, and in beginning to plan our wedding during the first year they were legal in our state, I observed something then that's still true today: Even with all the accomplishments and strides toward equality, the wedding industry is still incredibly heteronormative, and many same-sex couples feel it isn't speaking to them.

I'd seen the planning books that existed for straight brides and had an idea. I pitched it and had my Carrie Bradshaw moment when I got a book deal to publish the very first wedding planning book specifically for gay grooms. It was an interesting process to write it while being an engaged groom. It was never intended to be about the fight for gay marriage but a how-to book with a different tone and style, as it was intended for gay men. As a first-time author, I learned you get a team to help you, including an agent, a publishing house, an editor, and a graphic designer. This was all new territory, and we had some disagreements, including their decision for the title of the book not to permanently live on the cover. "What if a gay person wants to carry this around and not advertise that they're planning a wedding?" they asked. I regret not putting up a bigger fight for what I knew was right.

After *Getting Groomed* hit the shelves, four big things happened: (1) I left Soho House to begin working full time as a wedding planner, (2) same-sex marriage was legalized across our entire country, which was much bigger than my career, (3) we had an election in 2016 that I still haven't recovered from, and (4) after a four-year run, my husband and I decided to divorce. It was truly for the best and has only strengthened my understanding with couples about how challenging a marriage can be. I've moved on so fully from that marriage that I thought about not mentioning it here, but it's a part of my story, I don't regret it, and I believe fully that there should be no shame in divorce. It also gave me the push to go out on my own.

In 2017, I knew it was time for me to be in charge, and I launched Jason Mitchell Kahn & Co. I also learned that the publisher I used

MY AUDITION

would no longer be printing any more copies of *Getting Groomed*. The book industry is about numbers, and despite my book's great reviews, it was always compared to its counterparts for straight women, and there simply weren't as many gay grooms out there to buy it and keep numbers up. But as far as my business, from the very beginning our clients have mainly been people who identify as LGBTQ+ and some really creative and theatrical types who connect to me from my roots in theater.

After a little more than two years in business, something known as the pandemic hit us. It was a roller coaster for the wedding industry, but I always knew weddings would come back, and they certainly did! The way all the rescheduling happened, I did twenty-one weddings in 2021, with eighteen of them happening between Labor Day and Thanksgiving. Sometimes we had three per weekend! It was a stressful time as we navigated ever-changing requirements and new products, such as trailers for on-site rapid testing that came with a string quartet, but I was lucky enough to observe the most beautiful thing during that time. Weekend after weekend, I observed families seeing each other for the first time in a year and a half, friends sharing meals at big tables again, and people letting loose on the dance floor. After those simple pleasures had been restricted, the appreciation for their return was sublime.

My company has grown every year since then, and constantly meeting couples to work with whom I really feel a connection to has continued to make the job incredibly gratifying. From my theater perspective, there's no such thing as perfection. While many couples have thanked me for making their day perfect, I look at every one I've planned and ask, "Is there something we could've done better?" So, in asking that question after hundreds of weddings, I feel like I have a lot more to share with all of you. And that's why I felt it was time to write this book.

Thank you for indulging me on our first date. While this book might not be the near one thousand pages I devoured of Barbra Streisand's memoir, the rest is about the two of you and the story we're going to create together.

Now that you've read my audition, do you accept my offer to play this role in your wedding planning journey? If your answer was the title of this book, then let's get this show on the road!

ENDNOTES

1. Joan Rivers (@Joan_Rivers), "Any straight person complaining about the Supreme Court striking down DOMA should be forced to hire a heterosexual wedding planner," Twitter (now X), June 26, 2013, https://x.com/Joan_Rivers/status/349929513859284992.
2. AMC Theatres, "AMC Theatres. We Make Movies Better," YouTube, September 8, 2021, video, 1:00, https://www.youtube.com/watch?v=KiEeIxZJ9x0.
3. Oliver Hilmes, "Gay Life Flourished in Berlin Before Nazis Snuffed It Out," Advocate, February 15, 2018, https://www.advocate.com/commentary/2018/2/15/gay-life-flourished-berlin-nazis-snuffed-it-out.
4. Matt Mullen, "The Pink Triangle: From Nazi Label to Symbol of Gay Pride," History.com, last modified June 3, 2024, https://www.history.com/news/pink-triangle-nazi-concentration-camps.
5. United States Holocaust Memorial Museum, "Paragraph 175 and the Nazi Campaign against Homosexuality," Holocaust Encyclopedia, last modified May 4, 2021, https://encyclopedia.ushmm.org/content/en/article/paragraph-175-and-the-nazi-campaign-against-homosexuality.

Chapter 1

WRITING YOUR SCRIPT

"Where do we even begin with creating our show?"

Just about every couple I've ever worked with has asked me that very question. You're not alone. Let's start at the very beginning; it's a very good place to start, as they say (and sing). Every great script once began as just a thought in a writer's head and blank page. I'm here to push you to lay the foundation for your story. Whether you identify as someone who's type A or type B, left- or right-brained, demure or brat, it's time to embrace being something you may or may not be accustomed to: versatile. That's right, the key to this first phase is knowing that not only can two things be true, but two key concepts can happen at the same time: dreaming and organizing. I believe in you; you *can* do both simultaneously.

This book is designed to make your planning foolproof and fun. The biggest mistake you can make is jumping ahead and working on all the smaller details before the bigger picture is established. While not every wedding follows the exact same chronology in planning, we want to lay a solid foundation.

I warn you now that there will be temptations along the way. You can be harmlessly trolling on Instagram an ex who married someone else, and the next thing you know your whole feed is filled with branded cocktail stirrers that you then order on sale before we've even developed your beverage menu. One step at a time.

There's one golden rule you must agree to plan by: THERE ARE NO RULES. That's the fun and opportunity to make this personal. The reality in America is that to get married, all you have to do is sign a license. There's not one instruction from the marriage bureau that says, "This license will be deemed valid only if the two people who signed it also walk down an aisle, exchange rings, and have a first dance." And for those of you not marrying in our country, trust me, the same rules apply. The legal requirements for getting married are not associated with what ensues at the wedding.

Now, you may be thinking, "No rules? Endless options? How overwhelming!" Breathe. Break out those cocktail stirrers you accidentally ordered and have a cocktail or mocktail. Relax. I've got you.

DREAMING

If you've already dreamed up a decent picture in your head of what your wedding might look and feel like, then you're one step ahead. For those who are still on the blank page with the flashing cursor, let me start by asking you some key questions:

- Do you picture a ceremony followed by a reception?
- Do you picture all your close friends and family present?
- Do you picture religion being incorporated in any way?
- Do you picture exchanging vows?
- Do you picture the vibe to be more formal or casual?
- Do you picture this in the city you live in, grew up in, or somewhere different?
- Do you picture being outdoors for any part of the event?
- Do you picture being somewhere modern, old-worldly, rustic, or industrial?
- Do you picture a meal where everyone is seated and served at the same time?

WRITING YOUR SCRIPT

- Do you picture more of a cocktail-style party where there's plenty of food but isn't a formal meal service or assigned seating?
- Do you picture a crowded dance floor?
- Do you picture what you might wear?
- Do you picture entering by being lowered in a bubble from a fly-system and greeting all your guests by saying, "It's good to see me, isn't it?"

Okay, maybe that last one is my dream and not yours. But as you ask yourselves these questions, I need the two of you to complete an assignment: Sit down separately and write down (or type, dictate, make code with emojis) everything that comes to mind when you dream of your "once in a lifetime" event. Don't censor yourself. Just because it makes this list doesn't mean it's going to happen. We can't all arrive by boat to a waterfront ceremony, but if you've dreamed of it, at least write it down. Something like that might get scrapped once you start making budgetary decisions, but at least you put it out there as a possibility.

If this task already seems daunting, let me list and briefly explain some common elements of a wedding and where some of these traditions were born. I call them **The A to Z's of Wedding Components**. Right now I'm just going to highlight some of them for you. For ease of reference, and because I'm a lover of both dreams and organization, I alphabetized this list. But as you make your way through this book and every subject it covers, you'll discover there's not a one-size-fits-all chronology to planning a wedding. Therefore, this list is certainly not in the order we're going to work on together, and for now these are just broad strokes. But I encourage you to read (or at least skim) through all components. Then, as you start working on the action items related to each chapter, you can revisit this list to focus more on the details. As a reminder, none of these are required to be married, and you're just dreaming at this point. Try not to get hung up on the details, but as you read each item in the list, ask yourself whether it appeals to you.

■ ACTIVATIONS

Activations are what we at Jason Mitchell Kahn & Co. refer to as additional activities for guests to participate in. Commonly known ideas are photo booths and caricature paintings, but we've also seen henna stations, haikuists, and what has become a staple at many JMK weddings—a wig bar!

■ AFTER-PARTY

At some point the wedding reception must end, and if you know you're the type who won't want the party to end, an after-party might be important to you. We've planned some that were as elaborate as the wedding itself and others that were as simple as getting a bar reservation for a group back at the hotel where most guests were staying.

■ BACHELOR & BACHELORETTE PARTIES

Each individual's best person typically organizes the bachelor and/or bachelorette parties, and each includes the respective sides of the wedding party. They can be full weekend getaways to locations known for allowing debaucherous behavior, or they can just be a night out in your hometown. Most people in attendance pay their own way and then contribute to parts of the experience for the person getting married. Many JMK couples have had a joint party or weekend because they don't necessarily have defined sides.

■ CEREMONY

The ceremony is the main event, and no matter what takes place during it, it concludes with a couple being pronounced as married. The customs of ceremonies vary tremendously, often based on religion and culture. There are far too many to discuss in this book, but I promised to be inclusive, so I've included an appendix for those of you who are interested in learning more about some of them. Whether you're seeking to include religion in your ceremony or not, you might be surprised to learn that there are, in fact, nontraditional options and that most of what we know to be wedding customs aren't mandated anywhere.

■ COLOR PALETTE

A color palette is a combination of colors selected for various areas of your wedding, such as graphic design, event décor, and wardrobe of the wedding party. Choosing a color palette was once considered the starting point for designing weddings, and while many couples still like to have one to unify their vision, plenty of couples don't select one and still have beautiful events.

■ COUPLES' ACCOMMODATIONS

Many couples need to decide where they'll be sleeping on their wedding night, and it's important to consider this in advance because it can be a big-ticket item in the budget and affect decisions such as the location for getting ready.

■ DANCES

Several special dances can take place during wedding receptions. They range from the couple's first dance and parent–child dances to the money dance, the conga, and the shuffle. There are also traditional ethnic dances ranging from the hora, tarantella, ceilidh, and halay to the mezinka, hasapiko, and kalamatiano.

■ DATE

Your event will need a concrete date and time to take place. For some, this is very important because they want to create what will become a numerically significant anniversary, while others seek just a time of year or day of the week. Some don't care at all! You also might be at the mercy of when your favorite venue is available, so be cautious of getting married to a date first.

■ Décor

Your venue might be stunning by itself or need a major lift to fit your style. You might want to simply elevate it or completely transform it. We've turned exterior locations into enchanted gardens and interiors into speakeasies with hidden doors.

■ Destination Wedding

Not to be confused with an elopement, a destination wedding is one hosted somewhere other than where you live, often in a vacation-like setting, and all guests are asked to travel and stay there. From villas in Italy and castles in the South of France to a beautiful beach in the tropics, there are limitless possibilities throughout the world. As they usually require some effort for your guests to get there, it's customary for destination weddings to have several events over a few days.

■ Engagement Party

Engagement parties began as an old tradition thrown by the parents of the bride to announce the engagement and to let future wedding guests get to know each other. We certainly don't live in those times anymore, but for many these parties still happen. For some parents, it's a chance to do something in their hometown if their children won't wed there and they'd like to include some local guests who won't be invited to the wedding. Many couples also opt to throw an engagement party for themselves. If you're having a small destination wedding, an engagement party can be an opportunity to celebrate with some guests who won't be at the wedding. It can take place anywhere, from someone's home to a venue lavish enough for a wedding. It's also 100 percent not required to have one of these.

WRITING YOUR SCRIPT

■ EVENT PLANNER

While this book is written to empower you to do the job on your own, you might prefer to have an event planner take the reins. Event planners are available to help you with the entire process from start to finish, just to run the show on the day of, or some combination in between. There's an important distinction between a planner and the coordinator that comes with a venue. I can't tell you the number of couples who've told me they don't need a planner because their venue comes with a coordinator. This is not the same job! An event planner's primary concerns are the couple and every aspect of the event, while a coordinator's primary concern is the venue.

■ FAREWELL BRUNCH

In the vein of nuptials creating a "wedding weekend," it was common for a newly married couple to host a send-off brunch the morning after their wedding. Generally, these brunches are paid for either by the set of parents who hosted the rehearsal dinner or by the couple to say thank you. Many JMK couples have opted to host something later in the day that's not technically brunch but more of a recovery party.

■ FAVORS

Take-home favors are a way to enhance the guest experience by giving them something to enjoy after the event. These can be set at each place setting, passed out during the night, or displayed for guests to grab before they exit.

■ FLORAL DESIGN

Flowers have been incorporated into wedding design since as far back as we have photo evidence of these events. They often surround the area of the ceremony, are placed on every table at the reception, and are used as personals in the forms of bouquets and boutonnieres.

■ Food & Beverage

You must wine and dine your guests! A common format includes a cocktail hour that might have passed appetizers and/or some food stations, followed by a reception with a dinner that's usually a minimum of three courses. The entire night could offer an open bar including all spirits, wine can be served tableside at dinner, and champagne can be made available throughout the night as well as passed upon arrival or before a toast. It's also common to offer specialty cocktails or mocktails that have significance to the couple or to rename existing drinks to something about the couple. Late-night bites are also popular for refueling your guests.

■ Furniture

At nearly every venue, you'll have decisions to make about furniture. At certain places, every table, chair, and piece of lounge furniture must be rented. Others have furniture included, but you might find it's not your style.

■ Gift Registry

Gift registries were born in 1924 as a way for engaged couples to communicate their desired gifts to their guests. The online world has made registries a piece of cake to manage. Many couples have moved away from physical gifts and opted for guests to contribute to their honeymoon or raise money for charities that are important to them.

■ Graphic Design Assets

Also referred to as "day-of stationery," graphic design materials are commonly used in weddings, including ceremony programs, place cards, cocktail signs, and menus. Each can be designed in the same style as your invitation or independently. For some time these were always printed for the event, but now some couples have moved to having everything available digitally.

WRITING YOUR SCRIPT

■ GUEST LIST

It might sound obvious, but a guest list consists of all the people you plan to invite. When you first draft this, it helps inform you of the approximate number your venue needs to hold.

■ HAIR & MAKEUP

Do you want professionals handling hair and makeup for you, your wedding party, and your families? And this isn't exclusive to women; tons of my male clients have also wanted their appearances enhanced for the big day.

■ HONEYMOON

A honeymoon is the trip taken by newlyweds after the wedding. In olden days, the couple would leave toward the end of the reception to catch a late train or ship. Now most couples wait, whether it's just a few days to tie up loose ends from the wedding festivities or longer if it works best for the couple's schedule. Like any trip, locations vary based on personal tastes, but couples should always make sure they're booking somewhere that will be welcoming and supportive. If you'd like to take your honeymoon right after the wedding, be sure to plan this ahead of time in tandem with the main event.

■ HOTEL ROOM BLOCK

When you're inviting guests from out of town to attend a wedding, it's common to select one or a few hotels close to your venue where they can stay. You can arrange a discounted rate with the hotel because you're ensuring a certain amount of business. Guests can still choose to stay elsewhere, but this eliminates the work of them having to research where to stay. These can come either as a "courtesy block" in which you have no financial obligations if the block isn't completed or a "contractual block" in which you do.

■ INVITATIONS

If you want guests to attend, you must invite them. I'm sure that sounds obvious, but this used to be a very formal process handled by the set of parents who were paying for the event, and calligraphers were hired to hand-address each envelope. Modern times have introduced many more options, including invitations coming directly from the couple, and some forgo the printing process and do everything digitally.

■ LIGHTING & SOUND

Also known as AV, sound and lighting need to be arranged at your venue. This can be as minimal as providing amplification for an outdoor ceremony, or it can involve renting an entire lighting system to enhance your event design. If your venue has any AV restrictions or requirements, it's imperative you understand them.

■ LINEN

Linen makes an impactful part of the wedding design because guests get a close view of the cloth on the table they're sitting at and the napkin they put on their lap. There's a huge range of what they can look like, feel like, and cost.

■ MARRIAGE LICENSE

Getting a marriage license is the one must-do if you want to legally marry. It's the document the two of you and your officiant sign to make the marriage official. The requirements and process to obtain one vary state by state. Some require you both to go in person with identification and require two witnesses to also sign, while others have fewer rules. Typically, after the license is signed on the day of the wedding it gets mailed back in, and the couple receives a certificate of marriage within a few weeks. For the record, I've worked with several couples who, for a variety of reasons, have married in advance of the wedding, and the event still looks and feels the same to guests.

■ Music

A wedding of any kind needs musical entertainment, whether it's a full band, a DJ, or someone to operate a custom playlist. It's also popular to book additional musical accompaniment for the ceremony, such as acoustic guitarists or string quartets.

■ Officiant

If you're having a ceremony, someone needs to lead it. Traditionally this was a religious figure such as a priest or rabbi. Now couples have the option of a variety of officiants, from a justice of the peace to a best friend who gets ordained for the occasion.

■ Performances

Performances are different from the main musical act you might book. Are you interested in having a special appearance by a singer, a drag queen, an aerialist, or a go-go dancer? Those are just a few examples of the various types of talent we've added to some of our weddings.

■ Personal Styling

Stylists can help couples feel their best for the big day in a few ways. During the planning, they can help source and suggest any component of the wardrobe or accessories that feels daunting, and they can also be hired to be on hand throughout the wedding to ensure every part of the garments you're wearing are always in the right place.

■ Photography & Videography

Documenting your special day is important. As I've said to many couples, it's the element of the wedding you really can take with you. Besides a wedding planner, photographers and videographers are the vendors who are around you the most, so it's important you like not only their work but also their vibe. Many couples also have an engagement photo shoot before their wedding, which allows a couple to get to know their photographer and grow more comfortable in front of the camera.

■ REHEARSAL

The day before the wedding, it's typical to have a rehearsal of the ceremony with everyone who's participating in it. This is a chance for anyone involved, such as those walking down the aisle, doing readings, or offering up the rings, to learn where and when they need to fulfill their responsibilities. *You* may have all the pieces committed to memory, but your sister-from-another-mister or good ol' Uncle Kevin may be wandering around like a lost puppy, and no one wants anyone to go rogue. Keep in mind that rehearsals rarely take place at the same location as the ceremony, and sometimes they take place at the back of a restaurant or in someone's large living room. So when they do get to be in the same place, it's a bonus!

■ REHEARSAL DINNER

The name of this event came from the fact that it usually commenced the night before the wedding, after the rehearsal. Traditionally this was given by the set of parents not paying for the wedding, though now the cost of both the rehearsal dinner and the wedding are often evenly split or paid for by the couple. The etiquette is to invite the wedding party, family, and all out-of-town guests. Many couples now choose to do this as more of a cocktail-style event, which we refer to as a welcome party. We also often break this into two tiers, where the night might begin with a more intimate family dinner followed by a party where more guests are invited.

WRITING YOUR SCRIPT

■ Rings

Rings used to always be the pieces of jewelry that accompanied a proposal, then each person in the couple would also exchange wedding bands during the ceremony. Now there are countless other ways of making an engagement official, and if you're a couple who enjoy selecting paint swatches together, the same might be true for a ring. There are also several designs of two rings that interlock, so you essentially get half during your engagement and complete the look on your wedding day. And if you think rocks are more suited for cocktails, you can select new watches, bracelets, tattoos, or even a painting for your home. I had one couple exchange harnesses! The choices are endless as long as it's your style and looking at it daily reminds you of how your relationship has progressed.

■ Save the Dates

Often evoking a chuckle because the acronym is "STDs," save the dates come before the invitations so your guests can mark their calendars and begin to make travel arrangements. Just like invitations, these can be extravagant pieces of stationery, postcards, or simple online notices.

■ Showers

Traditionally, wedding showers have existed as a custom for brides-to-be. They're generally an afternoon event hosted by the bride's closest friends or parents where guests bring gifts and offer the woman advice before she enters married life. This custom doesn't generally translate for grooms, but in our world of no rules, have a shower if you're a groom and want one!

■ Social Media

In case you've been living underground like Kimmy Schmidt, social media platforms include Instagram, Tik Tok, Blue Sky,

Threads, X, and Facebook, just to name a few at the time of writing this. Some couples create new accounts just for their wedding content, while others have a strict no-posting privacy policy. If having your wedding go viral is important to you, there are also vendors you can hire specifically for capturing real-time content creation.

■ TABLETOP RENTALS

For any meal, guests will need plates, silverware, glassware, and more. Just like furniture, your venue might include the basics, but you can rent more custom items. Do you already know what a charger is? If not, you'll learn before finishing this book.

■ TENTS

Outdoor tents are a necessity for guaranteeing you can use the space you want despite the weather. They can be quite costly, especially if you want them to look nice in addition to being functional, but they're very important to consider as a part of a rain-or-shine plan! Some venues also require a catering tent for where the food will be cooked.

■ TOASTS & SPEECHES

During the reception, it's common for the parents or another important relative to give a welcome toast or blessing over the bread and/or wine. Other toasts throughout the event can include the other parents, siblings, best man, and maid of honor, and one is given by the newlywed couple.

■ TRANSPORTATION

Transportation should be considered not only for you but for your wedding party and your guests. It's common to arrange guest transportation if they're required to change locations or go somewhere difficult to find or park at. Rideshare apps have helped take the pressure off this always being a necessity, but you must consider their reliability where you're having the wedding. Having specialty transportation for both of you from the getting ready space to the venue is a fun way to further enhance the day, from vintage cars and stylized pedicabs all the way to a hot air balloon.

■ Venue

The venue is the location where you host the wedding, and sometimes the reception and ceremony are at separate venues. Common options are churches, synagogues, barns, warehouses, hotels, museums, country clubs, and ballrooms. Some venues handle all your needs for a wedding, and some require that you bring everything to the venue.

■ Wardrobe

You must wear something on the day of! The canvas of wedding fashion has grown so much wider than tuxedos and gowns. As you'll soon learn, it's all about identifying your style.

■ Wedding Cake

The custom of wedding cakes dates back to the Roman Empire but is now interpreted in a variety of ways. It used to be standard that the cake was large enough to serve all guests and had a topper that represented the couple. Traditionally, the couple makes the first slice, and they often save the top tier to consume it on their first anniversary. Many couples now forgo having a large wedding cake and cut into a small one just for the ritual, and some choose not to follow this tradition at all.

■ Wedding Party

Originally called a bridal party, a wedding party includes the friends and family the couple has chosen to honor in their wedding. Couples often consider what they want for the look of their wedding party, and members are meant to serve as additional support during the planning process and on the day of.

■ Wedding Website

Creating an online hub for all relevant wedding information has become standard now, and there are several companies that offer this service for free and with user-friendly templates. Wedding websites are a wonderful place to list all the information that doesn't fit on the invitation or perhaps isn't finalized by the time the invitations go to print. They allow guests to read in more detail about subjects such as where to stay, whether travel is being provided, what to wear, and where the couple is registered.

■ Welcome Bags

If you have guests coming in from out of town and staying in a hotel, it's customary for them to be greeted with an arrival gift. It begins their experience of your wedding weekend. These gifts can include light refreshments for the room, small tokens representative of the location, and a reminder of the weekend's itinerary.

ORGANIZING

Now that you've familiarized yourself with the dreaming stage of wedding planning and all its components, let's dream the dream not in time gone by but in more detail, then we can begin to organize it. I recommend that both of you complete the following assignment individually and then compare.

Based on the list I provided, it's time for you to rate, rank, and remove the items as you see fit. I've learned priorities are different for everyone. I've had couples tell me the dinner aspect is not super important to them and that if the food isn't offensive it will be fine, while other couples have introduced themselves to me as foodies

WRITING YOUR SCRIPT

and required a Michelin star-rated meal. Some couples care most about a venue with views, some tell me they need the best band in town to perform, and some tell me they want to hear only the original artists of their favorite music so a DJ is the only way. I once worked with a groom who was obsessed with furniture, so his number one priority was getting the right chairs brought in.

Since we need to assess what *you* want and need, we'll need a bit more detail than "Shantay you stay" and "sashay away." I recommend the following grading system:

- **DY = Definite Yes!** Can I get a yassss kween? No ifs, ands, or buts, we are having this at our wedding.
- **LY = Lean Yes.** I can picture this at our wedding and feel inclined to have it, but I haven't been obsessing about it like the presale for Beyoncé's next concert.
- **M = Maybe.** Take me or leave me, baby, I'm good either way.
- **LN = Lean No.** This doesn't make me cringe, but I'll sleep okay at night without it.
- **DN = Definite No.** Hard pass. Swipe left. Bye gurrrl bye!

To complete this and several other tasks outlined throughout this book, you have access to download our customizable wedding workbook, which includes a tab for each wedding component so that all information can live in one place. Most chapters throughout this book also include one or more samples you can use as a guide for organizing your process. It would be impossible to create a workbook that perfectly suits every couple, which is part of why we designed it as an online document with video tutorials. It's meant to be malleable to each couple's needs and wedding, and we update it regularly. At the moment it isn't customary to preview your wedding design through augmented reality tools.

Scan to download the workbook.

However, if that becomes an industry standard, we will certainly add it to our workbook.

To start, please download the workbook and draw your attention to the first three tabs: Wedding List for Person 1, Wedding List for Person 2, and Wedding List Mutual. Each of you should complete an individual list, then it's time for a conversation about compromise. While it's okay if you differ to some degree about certain elements, if this exercise concluded with the two of you wanting two totally different weddings, you have two choices:

1. Compromise for a more unified and solidified vision.
2. Have two weddings!

Don't forget you both must be willing to meet somewhere in the middle here. Unless you have an unlimited budget, which we'll get into in the next chapter, you can't have everything. If there are several items where one of you is a DY and the other a DN, you might need some professional intervention. Ask yourself whether you can live without this element. If not, what can you give up in exchange? What means more to both of you: getting coupled in couture or dining with Dom Perignon? Remember: Wedding diplomacy is not just the first step to a fabulous opening night but also what sets up your show for a long run.

Once you've compared your lists, made notes, scratched off a few things, and compromised like members of the democratic senate, you must create a Mutual Ranking System List. Number all items up for consideration in order of the importance you've mutually agreed to. Your list can evolve over time as you delve deeper into the wedding, but this order of priorities is good to look back at if you find yourself doubting last-minute choices. As we develop your budget and you see how much things really cost, some items may decrease in importance for you. That's normal, but at least declare them now. Here's an example from a recent JMK couple, who compromised quite a bit until they were on the same page:

WRITING YOUR SCRIPT

MUTUAL DY, LY, M, LN, DN

WEDDING ITEM	RANKING	ORDER OF IMPORTANCE	NOTES
Activations	LY	13	Would like a photo booth if budget allows
After-Party	DY	6	We both won't want the night to end
Bach Party	M	N/A	Fine if our friends organize something; but we're both in our forties!
Ceremony	DY	N/A	Obviously we're having one, but unsure what it will look like
Color Palette	M	N/A	Doesn't really feel like us
Our Accommodations	DY	12	We know we'll want room service in the morning
Dances	LY	N/A	Probably with our parents, but no first dance for us!
Date	M	N/A	Doesn't matter when as long as we like the venue
Decor	LY	9	Want it to look nice, but prefer simplicity
Destination	DN	N/A	We want to get married in our city
Engagement Party	LN	N/A	If our parents feel inclined to organize something
Event Planner	M	11	If we can afford this
Farewell Brunch	DN	N/A	We loathe these
Favors	LN	17	Feels wasteful and unimportant
Floral Design	LY	10	Will want some but simple is best for us

CONTINUED →

RANKING SYSTEM

RANKING SYSTEM

WEDDING ITEM	RANKING	ORDER OF IMPORTANCE	NOTES
Food & Beverage	DY	4	We want great food and a really nice bar offering
Furniture	M	15	I suppose we should, only if we don't like what comes with the venue
Gift Registry	LN	N/A	Really just want money
Graphic Design Assets	LY	14	Would be cool to have something custom with our initials
Guest List	DY	N/A	We want everyone we love to be there!
Hair & Make-Up	DY	8	We are not doing this without a professional getting us ready!
Honeymoon	DY	16	Unsure as to when, but definitely want a trip to celebrate at some point
Hotel Room Block	DY	N/A	Our guests will be clueless if we don't suggest where to stay
Invitations	LY	19	We know we need, but happy to keep simple or maybe do digital
Lighting & Sound	M	18	Depends on what will be best in venue
Linen	M	20	Only if needed
Marriage License	DY	N/A	We would like to make this legal!
Music	DY	2	Having a great band is what we're most excited about!
Officiant	M	N/A	Will ask a friend
Performances	DN	N/A	Doesn't seem like us
Personal Styling	DN	N/A	We can handle on our own
Photography & Videography	DY	7	We'll want to remember this night forever!

WRITING YOUR SCRIPT

WEDDING ITEM	RANKING	ORDER OF IMPORTANCE	NOTES
Rehearsal	M	N/A	Probably a good idea to have
Rehearsal Dinner	LY	21	We know our out of town family will expect something
Rings	DY	5	What color are the stones?
Save the Dates	DY	23	Can't wait to get the word out
Showers	DN	N/A	Games and little sandwiches are not our thing
Social Media	LN	N/A	Likely will ask people to be off their devices
Tabletop Rentals	LN	22	Will probably be fine with the basics
Tents	DN	N/A	Do not want anything outdoors!
Toasts & Speeches	DY	N/A	Can't wait to get roasted by my bestie!
Transportation	LN	24	Hoping hotel will be close enough to venue to avoid needing
Venue	DY	1	Want something really cool!
Wardrobe	DY	3	Want to feel like models for the day!
Wedding Cake	DN	N/A	Hate cake
Wedding Party	DY	N/A	We've been in enough of these and now it's our turn
Wedding Website	DY	N/A	We know this will make things easier
Welcome Bags	LN	25	Have never really understood the need for these

RANKING SYSTEM

As you determine your reasons for the order of this list, make little notes next to each item. Here are two examples in response to including welcome bags:

1. DY: I absolutely adore being greeted with these and love seeing what creative items the couple has chosen to include.
2. LN: I always throw these away before checking out of the hotel and couldn't care less about having another tote bag in my life.

Now that you've completed this exercise individually and as a couple, let me ask you two questions:

1. Do you have a clearer picture of what your dream wedding looks and feels like?
2. Do you feel like you've created a prioritized list so we can tackle the dream in an organized fashion?

If the answer to both is "We do," then you're ready to hit Save on the first draft of your wedding script and begin the least fun but super important next step. I'll see you there!

Chapter 2

THE PRODUCERS MEETING

Money makes the world go 'round, and it's crucial to determine what your wedding finances are before you spend a mark, a yen, a buck, or a pound. I say this as a type of vendor who would be nowhere if paying clients didn't exist. I'm a part of an industry, one that booms and blooms in the capitalistic society we exist in.

I've had many conversations with clients during which they've asked questions like, "I simply don't understand why renting new chairs costs that much." The truth of the matter is, a rental company with products like this can set their prices as they wish, and if there's enough demand to support them at that price point, they have no reason to charge less, even when you're as likable and charming as my clients tend to be. Vendors are also brands and, depending on their experience, can charge what they feel their work and time are worth, which may differ from their competition. More expensive doesn't always mean better, but you have to determine where you see value. A pair of Prada shoes are more expensive than a Steve Madden recreation, and only you can decide whether the more expensive one is worth it.

However, your special day should be one you look back at with fond memories, not as the event that diminished your savings account. The only way to accomplish this is to have a good understanding of two things from the get-go:

1. How much you have to spend, and
2. How much the wedding you want actually costs.

Let's start with the first question.

TARGET BUDGET

Determining your budget can be a little complicated depending on what your situation is with your family. There's no one-size-fits-all method for how this is handled, but there's a decent chance that if you were born female, paying for a wedding in some capacity, if not entirely, has been on your parents' radar. If you were born male, it's likely that paying for a wedding hasn't been on your parents' mind at all, even if you and your mother attended Cher's most recent, but hopefully not her last, farewell tour together.

I know the next task I'll be asking of you could potentially be triggering. Sadly, I've planned weddings for people with parents who refused to attend because they didn't accept their child for who they were and nor who they loved. Let me confirm for you: That is their loss.

For those of you who'll be getting financial support from your parents, you'll need to determine what that means. If your parents are ready to pop some bubbly with you, then I applaud them for being fabulous, but now it's time for you to tell them a little about the dream you solidified in chapter 1, then see how they'd like to contribute. If one of the reasons you're reading this book is because you have no idea what type of wedding suits you, chances are the apple didn't fall far from the tree. Your parents might be immediately forthcoming about what they're comfortable with, or they might come back to you with more questions.

Additionally, the two of you must decide how much of your own money you can and want to put into this. I've worked with plenty of couples who chose to pay for their wedding in its entirety because they felt it gave them more freedom to make the exact choices they wanted to. Everyone is in a different position.

If you've received exact numbers from both sides of the family and the two of you have assessed what you can comfortably add to the pot, you have what's known as your *target budget*. Ideally there's some flexibility with it as the project evolves; if there isn't any, and if there's absolutely no way you can put another single cent toward the wedding, then we refer to this as your *max budget*. Whether you have these numbers or they're still a work in progress, we must work on the other task simultaneously, which is figuring out what your wedding will cost.

ACTUAL BUDGET

Now, as much as I appreciate the internet for various bootleg recordings of old Broadway shows and other types of videos I usually watch in bed, the web can be misleading and unhelpful. There are articles written every year stating the "average price" of a wedding, which makes couples feel they can have an "average wedding" for that price. In this case, an average is a means between the most expensive and least expensive places you could wed based on where you live, but that number won't be of any use to you unless you truly reside somewhere that has a sweet spot right in the middle. As someone who's based in New York, I encounter so many people who feel they should be able to pull off a wedding here for much less than is feasible. I've planned weddings at all different types of price points, and I certainly don't believe you can only have a wedding if it costs a lot of money. But this exercise won't be useful if you aren't ready to understand what the actual cost will be for the type of wedding you want and where you want it to happen.

Don't fret if your ultimate number seems small based on what you've heard weddings cost. As we get into the following chapters and delve into selecting categories and components that have a price tag, I'll be sharing all sorts of JMK Tips for how to bring the costs down. For now, here's a breakdown of approximately how to allocate your ultimate number:

WEDDING BUDGET	% OF TOTAL
Reception Venue, Food & Beverages	40
Entertainment	10
Flowers, Décor & Sound/Lighting	10
Photography & Videography	10
Outfits & Rings	8
Tipping	6
Financial Cushion	4
Ceremony Venue & Officiant	2
Graphic Design Assets	2
Stylist (Clothing, Hair, Makeup)	2
Favors	2
Transportation & Parking	2
Cake	2

It's important to realize that these percentages are approximate because no wedding is the same. Think of this breakdown more as a malleable map when you start getting prices. You might select a venue with so much character it doesn't need flowers, so you can save that money or put it toward another wedding aspect. There's even a built-in financial cushion in case you go overboard with something!

Please observe that this breakdown does not include the cost of a wedding planner. If reading this book makes you realize you need someone like me, you'll definitely need to shift some of the guidelines to accommodate. We're an extremely important vendor to hire if you can't complete the scope of work yourself, just know that

THE PRODUCERS MEETING

some wedding planners charge a flat rate and others by percentage of the total project cost, which can be between 10 and 25 percent.

Over the years at Jason Mitchell Kahn & Co., we've developed a system that makes budgeting for a wedding transparent and allows you to make decisions from an informed place: We map out everything you're trying to achieve with educated estimates so that as you approve or decline an item in your budget, you understand how it affects the big picture. If you're using the workbook and scroll over to the budget tab, you'll see some samples attached to it, and the blank Master Budget Worksheet lists just about everything you could spend money on. There's also a guest count cell that's formulated to automatically adjust any of the per-person items, such as a catering package. This worksheet is designed to allow you to understand at any given time the lowest your wedding could possibly cost and the highest it could hit. Play around with understanding how totals might change if you end up with 100 guests versus 150. Here's one example:

WE DO

Guest Count: 203
Vendors to Feed: 18
Welcome Party Guest Count: 125
Target Budget: $225,000

MASTER BUDGET

			CONFIRMED FINAL
$ 97,096.62	**Venue**		
	Ceremony Fee	$	1,500.00
	Catering	$	60,900.00
	Vendor Meals	$	1,530.00
	Admin Fee (22%)	$	14,064.60
	Tax	$	6,922.02
	Gratuity	$	12,180.00
$ 20,850.00	**Band/DJ**		
	Reception, Ceremony Duo & Cocktail Trio	$	19,600.00
	Ceremony Audio		incl.
	Gratuity	$	1,250.00
$ 12,140.00	**Photographer**		
	(9 hours)	$	11,690.00
	Extra Hour	$	450.00
$ 4,600.00	**Videographer**		
	(6 hours)	$	4,600.00
$ 15,922.97	**AV**		
	Reception Lighting	$	12,825.00
	Outdoor Lighting	$	1,800.00
	Tax	$	1,297.97
$ 2,897.72	**Rentals**		
	Lounge Furniture	$	361.90
	Tax	$	32.12
	Delivery	$	256.04
	Catering Rentals	$	2,008.30
	Damage Waiver	$	56.13
	Tax	$	183.23

THE PRODUCERS MEETING

LOW ESTIMATE	HIGH ESTIMATE	NOTES
$ 1,500.00	$ 1,500.00	
$ 52,500.00	$ 67,500.00	175 (min) vs 225 guests
$ 1,020.00	$ 1,700.00	Projected 12–20 needed
$ 12,104.40	$ 15,554.00	
$ 5,957.29	$ 7,655.04	
$ 10,500.00	$ 13,500.00	
$ 4,500.00	$ 19,600.00	
$ 250.00	$ 1,250.00	
$ 6,500.00	$ 20,000.00	
$ 3,500.00	$ 10,000.00	
$ 10,000.00	$ 15,000.00	Party vibes please!
$ 0.00	$ 3,000.00	Do we need?
$ 0.00	$ 12,000.00	
	$ 2,040.00	
	$ 970.00	
	$ 2,008.30	
	$ 56.13	
	$ 183.23	

MASTER BUDGET

CONTINUED →

WE DO

MASTER BUDGET

			CONFIRMED FINAL	
$	28,477.81	**Flowers**		
		Ceremony, Tables & Personals	$	26,066.52
		Tax	$	1,411.29
		Deposit	$	1,000.00
$	2,185.00	**Wedding Cake**		
		For 200	$	2,035.00
		Pickup and Delivery	$	150.00
$	390.59	**Additional Activation**		
		Polaroid Camera Rental/Film	$	330.20
		Pens	$	9.84
		Notecards/Envelopes	$	50.55
$	3,151.80	**Hair & Make-Up**		
		Wedding Party Hair & Make-Up	$	2,550.00
		Gratuity	$	510.00
		Tax	$	91.80
$	3,853.54	**Printed Materials**		
		Save The Dates	$	920.00
		Save The Date Stamps	$	95.20
		Invitations	$	1,900.00
		Invitation Postage	$	220.00
		Programs	$	210.00
		Table Numbers	$	28.50
		QR Signs	$	18.00
		Escorts for Head Table	$	22.50
		Custom Napkins	$	184.00
		Card Box	$	35.59
		Cocktail Stirrers	$	219.75
$	7,800.00	**Transportation**		
		Shuttle Busses	$	6,500.00
		Gratuity	$	1,300.00

THE PRODUCERS MEETING

LOW ESTIMATE	HIGH ESTIMATE	NOTES
$ 15,000.00	$ 30,000.00	
$ 2,000.00	$ 3,000.00	
$ 150.00	$ 150.00	
$ 0.00	$ 330.20	
$ 0.00	$ 9.84	
$ 0.00	$ 50.55	
$ 2,000.00	$ 3,500.00	
$ 15.00	$ 920.00	Digital V Printed
$ –	$ 95.20	
$ 1,200.00	$ 3,000.00	Card Stock Variance
$ 220.00	$ 260.00	
$ 0.00	$ 210.00	
$ 28.50	$ 28.50	
$ 18.00	$ 18.00	
$ 22.50	$ 22.50	
$ 0.00	$ 184.00	
$ 35.59	$ 35.59	
$ 0.00	$ 219.75	
$ 4,500.00	$ 6,500.00	2 v 3
$ 900.00	$ 1,300.00	

MASTER BUDGET

CONTINUED →

WE DO

MASTER BUDGET

			CONFIRMED FINAL	
$	696.27	**Welcome Bags**		
		Tote Bag	$	340.82
		Popcorn	$	99.75
		Chips	$	52.70
		Cookies	$	161.91
		Water	$	21.11
		Advil – 2 per bag	$	19.98
$	448.73	**Take Home Favor**		
		Keychain	$	409.80
		Tax	$	38.93
$	1,920.24	**After Party**		
		Food – Platters	$	740.00
		Bar	$	750.00
		Tax	$	132.24
		Gratuity	$	298.00
$	26,367.21	**Welcome Drinks**		
		Passed Hors D'oeuvres	$	4,375.00
		Premium Open Bar	$	15,000.00
		Speaker/Microphone	$	300.00
		Admin Fee (5%)	$	983.75
		Tax	$	1,833.46
		Gratuity	$	3,875.00
$	4,000.00	**Couple Housing**		
		Thompson Suite for Weekend	$	4,000.00
$	232,798.50	**TOTAL**	$	232,798.50
		Both Sides Must Match		

THE PRODUCERS MEETING

LOW ESTIMATE	HIGH ESTIMATE	NOTES
$ 75.00	$ 340.82	Paper V Custom Totes
$ 99.75	$ 99.75	
$ 52.70	$ 52.70	56 pack for $52.70
$ 80.96	$ 161.91	12x2 packs for $17.99 – 1 per bag vs 2 per bag
$ 21.11	$ 21.11	
$ 19.98	$ 19.98	50 pack for $10.69
$ 0.00	$ 409.80	
$ 0.00	$ 38.93	
$ 740.00	$ 1,100.00	
$ 750.00	$ 1,500.00	Classic V Premium
$ 132.24	$ 230.75	
$ 78.30	$ 153.60	
		125–150 guests
$ 4,375.00	$ 5,250.00	
$ 15,000.00	$ 18,000.00	
$ 0.00	$ 300.00	AV for speeches maybe
$ 968.75	$ 1,177.50	
$ 1,805.51	$ 2,194.57	
$ 3,875.00	$ 4,650.00	
$ 2,000.00	$ 10,000.00	Basic Room V Suite
$ 164,495.57	$ 289,052.25	

MASTER BUDGET

Think of managing your budget as a project you'll be working on over time, not one for which you can lock down all costs up front. Also, as I tell all our clients, feel free to delete items up front that you know don't apply. For instance, if you select a venue and like the chairs they include, you can remove the line item for rental chairs. Or perhaps one of your parents has offered to pay for the reception and is planning to buy your wedding wardrobe, but they don't consider the latter part of the event budget.

Notice there are three columns that add up to total costs:

1. The low estimate
2. The high estimate
3. The confirmed cost

We typically fill out the estimates based on what we know to be true in the region where the wedding is taking place and what our clients want. There's a huge difference in a flower estimate if my clients want some simple bud vases on their tables versus those who want huge hanging installations. As you research venues and vendors, populate the estimates with what you discover. Once you know how everything contributes to the bottom line, you can assess things such as whether you can afford the photographer you like most or you need to find a less expensive one.

It's also important to think about tax and gratuities when you're analyzing your budget. These might seem like small numbers when you're buying the next round at happy hour, but they can become sizable figures when purchasing catering and an open bar for 150 guests. As you move on to the next chapters and begin to book different components of your wedding, make sure you thoroughly understand what's included and what's expected before you sign anything. Some venues that do in-house food and beverage service might simply require a minimum spend on food and beverage, and that number might seem very doable for your budget. However, be sure you calculate what your realistic spend will actually be. You might discover that the minimum cost of their food and drink multiplied by your guest count is triple your actual budget. Most food- and beverage-related contracts give you a number per person followed by a "plus plus," which refers to tax, gratuity, and any other required items, such as an admin fee. Some caterers or venues might include a service charge (which usually goes toward paying wages) plus a gratuity (the actual tip for the staff) that's often 18–25 percent of the cost per person. Some venues also require you to have event insurance and provide the required security and/or other staff members. I know venues that insist the coat check be staffed regardless of time of year and always include the fee for that person on the bill. Look for any hidden fees—they're usually in small print!

GUEST LIST

The final task of completing the budgeting element is to determine how many people you'll be paying for. Once that's done, I promise we'll take a break from number crunching until we discuss your waist size for the wardrobe.

Scroll over to the Guest List tab in the workbook and start filling in the Guest List Brainstorm Worksheet. For now, brainstorm all guests you could even consider. You'll see you can code them as either definite or maybe. While the worksheet will eventually be where you collect addresses and keep track of RSVPs, at this point you can just list first names or nicknames. Enter everyone you think you might invite, and don't censor! Nobody will see this list, so if your fourth cousin once removed is most likely a no but there's a small chance you'll change your mind, write them down so you don't forget. Here's what mine would look like:

WE DO

GUEST LIST

NAME ON ENVELOPE	ADDRESS 1	CITY
DEFINITES		
Carrie Bradshaw		
Miranda Hobbes		
Charlotte York Goldenblatt		
Harry Goldenblatt		
Samantha Jones		
Her Stockbroker from Season 6 (Name?)		
MAYBES		
Aidan Shaw		
Steve Brady		

THE PRODUCERS MEETING

STATE	ZIP	EMAIL	RVSP Y/N	NOTES

GUEST LIST

For the sake of budgeting and finding a venue, which is the next step, it's important to understand how many people you need to accommodate. It doesn't require an expert to tell you that if you fall in love with a place that can accommodate only one hundred people and your definite list is over two hundred, then the initial planning phase isn't going well. It's also important to remember that this list is likely to change by the time you're ready to invite people.

After your list is complete, go back to the vision you discussed after reading chapter 1. Did you both agree to keep this an intimate affair or to invite everyone you know? As you make this list, be sure to run through the following questions:

- Have you thought of every family member? Besides parents, siblings, and grandparents, have you remembered the aunts, uncles, and cousins? What about any of their children? Is this an adults-only affair?
- Are there any friends of the family to include such as neighbors, parents, coworkers, Dad's golf buddies, or Mom's martini gals? (Sometimes these people feel closer than actual relatives, and you might want to include them.) Depending on what your parents' financial contributions will be, do they have a list of invitees they want to include?
- Who do you want to invite from work? Who do you *have* to invite from work? Do you have any clients you need to include?
- What about all your social friends and acquaintances? Who are you still in touch with from college? Are there any professors who deeply impacted your life that you're still close with? Are there any friends from summer camp you still feel a connection with? Have you become close to anyone at the dog park? Did any exes actually turn into genuine friends?

When making this list, think about everywhere you spend any time besides work, such as the gym, bars, and restaurants or your cooking group, book club, or therapy group. If anyone feels like

THE PRODUCERS MEETING

someone you want to share a personal experience with, jot them down. As I said, you can always remove them after you have a panic attack about the guest count!

Now, take 40 percent of your ultimate budget number (the approximate cost of the venue, food, and beverages) and divide it by the maximum number of guests that will attend. This is the cost per person you'll want to strive for as you figure out the most expensive element of your wedding: the place and what you're serving your guests. If you're looking at venues that don't do in-house food and drink, back the cost of the venue out of the equation so you know what you're working with for caterers. Does your cost per person make it seem like all you'll be able to offer is a glassof water in a free park?

Below are some JMK Tips you can consider up front before you throw this book out the window.

JMK TIPs

Invite Fewer People

Reevaluate your guest list and take out those maybes. Many people have tiny weddings, and any true friend should understand why you might have a limited guest list. Personally, I feel living through a pandemic has made this an even easier path that does not require justification. You do you!

Try to Have the Ceremony and the Reception at One Place

By holding two components in the same location, you won't have to deal with transportation and various teams setting up in multiple places. It might even give you a leg up for negotiating.

Look for Venues That Are Inherently Beautiful and Filled with Character

While a venue with floor-to-ceiling windows might seem more expensive up front, those views might do all the heavy lifting for your design plan.

Look for a Venue Without a Site Fee

Try to find a location that doesn't have a site fee, or try to negotiate to have the fee waived. If a place does on-site catering, sometimes they'll remove their fee if you agree to spend a certain amount on food and beverages.

Have a Friend or Family Member Officiate the Ceremony

Having a friend or family member officiate the wedding not only makes it more personal but saves you the fee of a traditional wedding officiant.

Opt for a Day Other than Saturday

Saturday is the most popular day for weddings, as is holding them on a weekend during peak season. Many places offer lower fees for days or times of the year that are less popular, and they might even negotiate more if you're booking an "off" night.

Limit the Bar Offerings

Beverage packages can come with a very steep price tag, especially when they're offered as my favorite adjective for cocktails: unlimited. It can often save you a big chunk of change to offer only wine and beer or have an open bar available only during cocktail hour rather than the whole night. If your venue or caterer quotes a price per head for beverages, see whether you can avoid paying for those who won't be consuming, such as the sober, pregnant, and youth. And while we're discussing ways to save on drinks, say bye-bye to bubbles! Champagne toasts are a tradition you can forgo, especially since many people don't even care for champagne or will take one sip from the full glass you've paid for them to have. People can toast with any drink in their hand other than water, which is considered bad luck!

Have a Daytime Wedding
Brunch and lunch food is often considerably cheaper than dinner, and you can really limit the bar. An afternoon affair also comes with less pressure for entertainment.

Scale Down Your Menu
Not every wedding has to be a culinary journey. You might not really need a six-course meal with wine pairings followed by a wedding cake. Ask for less expensive menu items, look for a food package that includes the cake, and if cake isn't one of those wedding elements that's part of your dream, skip it. Maybe you can forgo having a caterer all together and opt for large format takeout served cocktail style.

Keep It All Inside
I know many people have dreams of being married in nature, but if you can't afford the rain plan for your setup, you really can't afford the wedding.

Reconsider the Entertainment You Dreamed Of
Bands are considerably more expensive than DJs. If you want additional musicians for your ceremony, try sourcing students from a local college music program.

Pay in Cash
Don't tell the IRS I suggested this, but if you're able to, see whether any of your vendors offer the option to be paid in cash. Florists, photographers, and some others might be able to lower their costs or not charge you tax if you do so.

> **Invite Online and Go Digital**
> You know what's cheaper than even the least expensive print shop? Not printing at all. Both your save the dates and your invitations can be sent digitally, and on the day of the wedding, rather than having programs and menus, guests can access this information through a QR code you create and have on display.

Congratulations! You've made it through the least sexy part about wedding planning. You've not only begun inputting numbers on a spreadsheet but have started the process of laying down the framework for your show. You've developed a vision for the story you want to tell and pitched it to the producers. If everything is aligning, you're ready to move forward. If not, you need to spend a little more time either refining the dream or chatting with the investors. For the sake of this analogy, that might be just the two of you and some family.

The workbook is your valuable tool for staying organized here. As you begin refining your guest list and zeroing in on your budget, revisit it as often as needed. Remember: The budget is an ever-evolving project that often isn't settled to the penny until after the wedding. What's most important along the way is that your target budget is somewhere below the high estimate for everything. If it rises above, either you must be okay with increasing the budget or something has to be removed to keep the number doable for you. You also need to accept that sometimes a budget increase is out of your control; something like global inflation can influence products such as food and flowers. Also remember that the whole process, not just the accounting of it, is an experience of change and growth. Simply put, you're allowed to change your mind about things along the way.

Okay mathletes, do you feel ready to take the next step? Because the sky's the limit! Or as Cady Heron from *Mean Girls* says, "The limit does not exist!"[1] I'll meet you where this event goes from dreams and spreadsheets to getting very real: the where and when!

ENDNOTE

1. *Mean Girls*, directed by Mark Waters (2004; Los Angeles, CA: Paramount Pictures, 2004) DVD.

Chapter 3

BOOKING THE THEATER

With a vision for your show and the financial greenlight, we now have the most crucial step in the planning process to take: finding a home. We all want to be in the room where it happens, but these big decisions are tough. Rest assured, you already made the biggest one by choosing to marry the person you love. Now you have the second-biggest decision to make: Where and when do you declare that love?

Every time I book a new client and we're at the dreaming stage, I emphasize how everything hinges on setting. Once a venue is booked and a date is set, the project goes from seeming hypothetical to "this is really happening." The informative factors of place and time will help you finish organizing the framework for the whole event. Once the foundation is solid, we'll work from the outside in to get every little detail in place. And the ones that follow from here will become easier and more fun, wedding planner's promise!

Whether time is more important than place or vice versa depends on you. Some people dream of a fall wedding, while others have their hearts set on a certain location. Which (if either) is more important to you? Start there. If you have a dream venue, the first step is finding out whether it's available. If your vision includes something outdoors, time of year is critical to consider. Maybe there's one season that calls to you or a specific numerical pattern of a date you want your anniversary to be for good luck. Which high priority on your list from chapter 1 might help specify your search?

Time of year may not be important to you because of what you're seasonally allowed to wear or what flowers are most in bloom, but the amount of time from now until the event is very important to consider. In my career I often feel like I've been through the wedding Olympics. I've planned weddings for over two years with a couple, navigated some couples' postponement to their fourth wedding date during the pandemic, and even planned a wedding from start to finish in forty-eight hours the first weekend gay couples could marry in New York. Truly anything is possible!

However, I'm here to keep you feeling calm and organized, so I don't recommend trying to plan all of this on an exceedingly truncated timeline. If you're envisioning a lot of the bells and whistles a wedding can have, I recommend nine months to a year. If you're going for something much simpler, you likely have more flexibility. Our wedding workbook includes a JMK Master Calendar, and there's a sample at the end of this chapter. I encourage you to read through it in detail and get a sense of how involved and time-consuming this process can be. Allow time for new ideas to develop as you plan, and don't spend every day feeling you're behind schedule. As you begin to inquire at venues, it's best to have an ideal date or a date range in mind. Sometimes couples will say to me, "We're truly open to anything."

I equate finding the right location for your wedding to finding real estate. If you've ever been in the market for a home or an apartment or have just watched a lot of *House Hunters*, you'll understand. You might walk into a place with tons of wow factors but not be able to picture yourself there. You also might be appalled, disgusted, or frankly frightened at what's shown to you based on its condition or

BOOKING THE THEATER

what's included. But just like selecting a new place to live, when you find the right place, you have an emotional reaction. Then you pray it's both available and affordable!

It's important to enter the location search with an open mind. Having organized this process for so many couples, I've heard countless times how the venue they fell in love with was nothing like they expected it to be. As with everything, it's important to keep your venue search as organized as possible. Toward the end of this chapter, I'll explain how to keep track of which places you've contacted, their availability, the costs associated with them, and how you felt after you visited each one. I've known some couples who booked the very first venue they saw, while others had to tour over twenty of them to feel confident in their decision. As you explore venues you might not be familiar with, feel free to talk to other couples who've wed there to get a sense of what their experience was like.

Now, back to the real estate metaphor. Depending on where and when you're trying to do this, it might start to feel very competitive. Popular venues can book out over two years in advance, but remember that there are many happy accidents that come with the planning process. If the place you love is booked the Saturday night you wanted it, it might cost considerably less on Friday or Sunday. I worked for a New York couple who really wanted a wedding in Provincetown, Massachusetts, because they spent their summers there and loved it, but with an expected guest count of four hundred there was simply no venue or accommodation option to make this feasible. We ended up with a waterfront venue in Brooklyn and let P-town serve as the design inspiration.

If you're getting married in the city or town you live in or close by, I encourage you to see as many venues as possible. If you're planning something out of town, schedule a trip when both of you can explore the options of that city. Remember: If you're inviting people who'll be traveling from out of town, you need to keep lodgings for them in mind. And if you're having a destination wedding, you'll want to find a place that you not only feel a connection to but can trust to handle most of the planning virtually.

PLACE

As I overuse the real estate metaphor in this chapter, you may start to realize it's all about location, location, location. Have tons of options for what theater can house your show? Let's explore the pros and cons of each type of venue.

■ RELIGIOUS VENUES

If it's important or significant to you to have your ceremony at a religious venue, make sure you feel comfortable there. There are synagogues and churches with exclusively LGBTQ+ congregations and some that still separate men and women. Religious venues tend to come with a ton of rules for having an event. For one, they often have very strict times when you're allowed to have the ceremony. Churches usually have a schedule with other programming, so often weddings are offered when they don't interfere with other services, or sometimes the wedding becomes part of the service and therefore might have other guests who attend. In most synagogues, you can't get married on Shabbat, which is Friday sundown to Saturday sundown. Your reception might also get off to a late start. If you want to have the ceremony in a place of worship and the reception elsewhere, just know it will increase the logistics you must plan for.

JMK TIP

If it's a rabbi or priest you're interested in, they'll often perform the ceremony elsewhere for a fee.

■ HOTELS

Holding your wedding at a hotel with an event space and suitable accommodations simplifies the logistics for your out-of-town guests. However, I stress that it's more important to fall in love with where the wedding will take place rather than with the rooms for guests. Some hotels are rich in character and have event spaces that need very little, while others have dated ballrooms that haven't changed their setup from conferences they had in the 1980s. If the event space and accommodations align, you can work with their reservations department to get a block of rooms at a discounted rate for your out-of-town guests. Often by doing this and hosting an event, you have the upper hand because you're providing multiple forms of business. Some hotels will even give the wedding couple a complimentary room.

The other factor to consider with a hotel is the catering or event manager you'll be working with. They can either be a wonderful resource for knowing what works best in the space and providing additional resources, or they can make it clear they are not flexible in how things are done nor interested in anything other than your check clearing. Because you'll be working directly with this person, it's important you feel you can work well together. And if you love everything about the way a hotel looks, try to taste their food before you book! Some hotels have incredible lobby restaurants but offer different food at events. If you get sample menus that don't excite you, try to gauge whether the hotel's catering staff can be accommodating.

Also, be sure to understand the traffic pattern and bathroom options, both for your guests staying at the property and for those who'll just be attending the event. Inquire about what other events could be booked at the same time. I was at a hotel once that had four weddings happening simultaneously!

JMK TIP

If you love the event space at a hotel but feel the rooms might be too high-end for some of your guests, you can always provide options of a few less expensive hotels nearby. If you love the location and rooms for your guests, the hotel could be an option for where you root the weekend but don't have the wedding. You could have supporting events there but provide transportation to a venue that feels more like you.

■ **COMMON VENUES**

Some venues, such as banquet halls, private clubs, castles, barns, and estates, are more exclusively used for weddings and other events. I'm referring to the ones that regularly seek to hold weddings. Some offer a wedding package that includes taking care of everything for you, from the catering to the tables. Other spaces are just a space, usually with a lot of rules and restrictions, and you must coordinate the rest. If you're considering the latter, you have to decide how much additional work, planning, and expenses you can and want to take on. A blank space where you have to bring in furniture, hire a licensed caterer, and hang lights could end up costing more than a venue that has everything available to you. Research past events that have taken place there, and try to connect with previous couples who'll relay their experience. Be sure to find out what's included when inquiring. I've toured venues with beautiful chandeliers, but having them on wasn't included, so couples were required to purchase a separate lighting package to use them. I've also worked at private clubs where members who aren't part of the wedding felt entitled to crash because it was "their club."

BOOKING THE THEATER

JMK TIP

If you don't want to feel like your wedding is a dime a dozen to the people you're giving business to, avoid booking a wedding factory.

■ RESTAURANTS

A restaurant you love for its cuisine, style, and vibe can be a fantastic option. You might not have to spend a dime on décor, and you know the food will be fabulous. If you love a restaurant and they're willing to host your private event, there are a few things to keep in mind. First, they'll expect you to at least match the revenue they'd take in from a normal night of business. Often clients will react to the price tag of a restaurant and feel that because they inquired about a wedding, they're being quoted something abnormally high. That's not true. If a restaurant typically turns their tables three times a night, their minimum is based on that projection regardless of whether you have only one meal service during your wedding.

Second, the seating arrangements might be limited to what's there, and you'll have to assess whether there's an option for a dance floor that's suited to you. You also might be required to cover some rentals to serve all your guests at the same time. Be sure to inquire about the music options, even if you're after something as simple as providing a playlist. If you're interested in just a section of a restaurant and not doing a complete buyout, be sure to keep other patrons in mind.

Third, evaluate the traffic patterns of the restaurant and see whether they can offer you a private feel. You likely don't want strangers passing through your reception to be seated at their table or to use the restroom.

JMK TIP

If you love a restaurant for its food and vibe but the space simply doesn't work, see whether they can offer off-site catering. I worked with a couple who loved a Michelin-star restaurant in their neighborhood that could seat only about forty people, so we brought the chef and his team off-site where they served some of the couple's favorite dishes to a guest count of 130 people.

■ **RAW SPACE**

Jokes about liking it raw aside, raw venues are truly nothing but space. They can be cool warehouses, lofts, courtyards, or studios, to name a few, but they don't come with most of what you'll need for a wedding. You might need to bring in lighting, flooring, and furniture just to make the space functional before you even get into design. The perk of raw spaces is that they often have the greatest amount of flexibility if you're really looking for this to be a creative endeavor. I don't recommend trying to pull this type of wedding off simply because you're a proud fan of *We Do*. You'll need a professional who can really manage the tremendous amount of detail that goes into selecting all the equipment you'll need, determining how and when it gets there, and overseeing all the components being set up simultaneously.

JMK TIP

If you love a raw space but its base cost eats up most of your budget, this is not the route for you. These types of weddings require a budget that can handle all elements.

■ OUTDOORS

Outdoor weddings are a favorite for some. There's no charge for beautiful views, existing foliage, or the sound of Leslie Uggams belting "June is Bustin' Out All Over," and natural lighting can be a photographer's greatest tool. However, if creating an enchanted forest for a ceremony or having an alfresco dinner is part of your vision, the downside is how little control you have over Mother Nature. Everything you arrange must have a plan B in case of bad weather or other unforeseen circumstances. Be honest with yourself here. Can you handle the uncertainty leading up to the big day? Does your venue have a reasonable rain option? Can your hair handle the humidity? Make sure your day won't be ruined if the weather doesn't cooperate.

There are regional differences here. When I first started planning weddings in Los Angeles, I was shocked that we didn't reserve rain tents. I've also seen Los Angeles weddings held when it was simply too hot for the guests to enjoy themselves outdoors and there was no inside component. I once planned a wedding in Boca Raton that was meant to include an outdoor dinner. We were relieved that week when the forecast showed no sign of rain. But while it did stay dry, the wind was so severe that the venue couldn't execute the tableside service, the décor planned for the tables would've been a mess, and we knew dressed-up guests would be uncomfortable.

> **JMK TIP**
>
> If you don't like or can't afford a weather contingency plan, an outdoor wedding isn't for you.

■ UNEXPECTED VENUES

The sky's the limit for less common venues, from museums, theaters, historic homes, and lofts to aquariums, wineries, piers, speakeasies, and more. I once had two grooms approach me who said their vision was to get married on unicorns, so we booked the next best thing and planned their wedding at a carousel in Brooklyn. We had only an hour to set up the entire event, which was inside a very busy park. To make it happen, we strategically and meticulously preloaded everything needed for the wedding, including chairs, lighting, bars, and beverages, into a giant U-Haul so we could unpack and get it all into place quickly and efficiently. So consider any place you feel drawn to and will allow you to host a wedding, but really chat through the logistics of your vision and make sure it can be comfortably executed. It's one feeling to have a wedding like no one has had before; it's another to feel like your event was an experiment gone wrong.

You may need to do very little to get the aesthetic you like, or you may need to do a ton to have a successful event. I applaud anyone who thinks outside the box and makes a daring choice for an event, but there are some important questions you must ask if this is your chosen route:

- Are there *enough bathrooms* for the guests?
- Do you need any *special permits* to have an event there?
- Do they allow you *enough set-up time* for an event? Do they charge extra for it?
- Does it have *proper air-conditioning or heating* to keep your guests comfortable during your chosen time of year?
- Does it have *suitable lighting and/or power* for an event, or will you need to bring some in?

- Can they *receive deliveries* properly? It's one thing for your guests to travel down a small staircase; it's another for tables and ice.
- Do they have a *kitchen* or a space where you can have a catering kitchen set up?
- Do they have an *on-site manager* who'll be there on the day as a point of contact?

JMK TIP

Don't sign up for an unexpected venue without having a professional involved. Even if you feel competent taking on that role, you'll still need someone who can be there on the day of to problem-solve should anything arise.

■ **PRIVATE RESIDENCE**

If you have a home being offered to you, this can be a lovely option for a variety of reasons: (1) If it's coming from a generous parent, other relative, or friend, there likely isn't a site fee attached, (2) it might be a place of sentimental connection to you, and (3) it probably isn't a place where most of your friends have attended other weddings. However, you must consider a few things. Is there any risk of damaging your relationship with the homeowner if anything happens to the property? Not every guest is always on their best behavior. And is it really a cost-saving option? Beautiful homes aren't typically designed to easily accommodate hundreds of guests, and even if there is space for them, you need to think about bathrooms, where food will be prepared, power supplies, and parking. By the time you bring in the infrastructure for everything you need, this option might be more expensive than another kind of venue.

>
> ### JMK TIP
>
> Noise is a factor you must consider. The last thing you want is uninvited neighbors reporting your wedding. If you're aware of any volume ordinances and feel the event can go off as planned, think about sending a little something to those neighbors in advance. A little gift and a note letting them know in advance goes a long way.

■ Destination Weddings

If your budget allows, there's always the option of a destination wedding. From castles in Scotland and villas in Italy to the beachfronts of Hawaii, there's no shortage of places that will make your wedding a truly transportive experience for you and your guests. It can also be a way for you to reduce your guest count a bit. However, you must bear in mind that any guests you'd like to have there will need to travel to your choice spot, and once they do, it's likely you'll be taking care of the rest. The larger your list gets, the more coordination you have to do. You might need to arrange everyone's transportation from the airport, plan activities for non-wedding festivities, and assist with navigating foreign customs.

You also have to take into account the fact that you'll be dealing with vendors local to your venue. A laid-back island feel might be what you want, but it can easily become frustrating when a vendor doesn't reply quickly to emails. If you find a dream spot in your travels, make sure you feel comfortable with its catering or event manager, especially since you'll likely be dealing with them via Zoom and email throughout the whole planning process. This means you must also prepare for the unexpected. The second wedding I planned in London threw me for a curve when a labor strike ensued that day and the Tube stopped running, preventing several of the employees of the venue from showing up for work! I also planned a wedding for two New Yorkers in Mexico, during which we discussed at length with the catering manager whether we could ship any items in advance. We were told that as long as they arrived in the country by a certain date, they'd be waiting for us, so we collected every guest's shoe size to create flip flops that would've left the imprint of the couple's initials on the sand. But they didn't make it out of Customs until four weeks after the wedding. Now, whenever we're producing anything in advance that's not being executed by a local vendor, we pack it and bring it ourselves.

JMK TIP

Be sure you understand a location's accessibility and how that might impact who from your guest list can attend. If a castle in a cobblestoned town that can be reached only by boat is calling to you, make sure you understand what your guests will need to go through to attend. This could potentially prevent certain guests from being able to commit, and that's a choice you must face. Remember, though, that you can always stream your ceremony to someone who can't make the journey.

TIME

If time is more of a deciding factor than place, let me give you some pros and cons to all times of the year, times of day, and days of the week. There used to be more popularity among some of these scenarios, but in the post-pandemic world a lot of that got thrown out the window, and we don't seem to have slow seasons anymore.

As I share a little insight about the times of year, some of this will not apply based on your location. Find what works best for you, and the rest will come!

■ SEASONS

I grew up in Florida and never even saw snow until I moved to New York. If you're planning something in an area you're not familiar with, be sure to look into weather trends and any other local occurrences that might be going on at the same time. If you ever try to plan a wedding in Palm Springs while Coachella is taking place, you'll discover that although there are plenty of venues, booking hotels for your guests is nearly impossible!

● Summer

Now, I'm a summer baby, and summer is my favorite time of year. I'm very happy when it's time for shorts and tank tops. But that's usually not the dress code for a wedding, so you must think about what your and your guests' experiences will be with the dress code you have in mind. "Sweaty Black Tie" is not a fashion description we usually publish on wedding websites, but that might be a moot point if your venue has proper air-conditioning. Be sure to ask, especially since it's easy to forget if you're looking in the winter. If it's a venue with views and all windows, know these places heat up like hotboxes. If you're planning anything outdoors, be prepared to have not only a rain plan but some insect repellent; being near water means being near bugs and humidity. Make sure you're always able to keep your guests hydrated and can provide shade for those who don't like the sun.

● Fall

If fall is speaking to you, it might be because it tends to be the sweet spot between extreme heat and cold. Many

JMK couples have said it's their favorite time of year because of the changing leaves and more pumpkin content than you could imagine. Just keep in mind that the weather can range from unseasonably warm to cold, and if anything is happening outdoors, you need to be sure you can keep your guests at a comfortable temperature. See whether your venue has heat lamps and if they'll charge you more to use them. There are many holidays in autumn, so also be sure to check the calendar and note what might cause conflicts for your guests.

- **Winter**

Winter is personally my least favorite season to exist in but the one I love to plan weddings in. It often gives you the most options for venues, and trying to schedule activations such as an outdoor photo booth becomes unnecessary. It's also a nice season for getting dressed up in luxurious fabrics and then being served a warm and rich meal. I strongly encourage having your ceremony and reception in one venue at all times of year, but particularly in winter. Be sure to inquire whether your venue will have holiday decorations up and whether they'll move them if you desire. I wouldn't want my guests entering a lobby filled with Christmas décor while holiday music plays on repeat . . . unless of course it's limited to Mariah Carey's "All I Want for Christmas Is You"!

- **Spring**

Spring was once considered the wedding season of all seasons, and it remains a popular choice. It's similar to fall in that it can still resemble the winter that has just passed or the summer that's on the horizon. Rain is common in the spring, so make sure there's a rain plan for anything outdoors and that there's a place for raincoats and umbrellas inside. Also check whether your venue has multiple events going on; there could be a competing wedding or, even worse, a prom!

■ DAYS OF THE WEEK

Saturday nights are the most common for weddings, so they tend to be the most sought-after, expensive, and competitive. But I've planned weddings on just about every day of the week, including many Mondays for Broadway couples, and it has never been a barrier for their non-theater guests to still attend. Point being, you don't need a Saturday to ensure a fabulous time and that everyone who truly wants to be there will be. Many people like Saturday so they can have a rehearsal dinner on Friday night and a brunch on Sunday before everyone travels back home. This is worth considering, but only if your dream involves having a three-day affair versus a single one.

I've also observed how much guests seem to love a Friday wedding, especially because after a Thursday through Saturday three-day shebang, Sunday is a built-in recovery day. Sundays are also a wonderful alternative for a wedding day. You can start earlier so it doesn't get too late for your more responsible friends. Holiday weekends, when most people get an extra day off work, are also good options for weddings. Especially when you have several out-of-town guests, a holiday weekend gives them an excuse to make a vacation out of coming to your wedding. However, they can also be weekends with conflicts for many. If anything you're throwing is on or around a holiday, be sure to verify the hours of all your vendors. Depending on the venue's demand, they might charge Fridays, Sundays, and holiday weekends identically to Saturdays.

■ TIME OF DAY

The time you have your wedding is another place where you can keep things more expected or opt for something different. My clients typically look at when sunset will be on the day of the wedding. If anything will be happening outside, it's often nice for the ceremony to still have sunlight, then for the sun to set during cocktail hour, then for it to be nighttime for dinner and dancing. However, this doesn't always work. I've planned many weddings in the summer when sunset is quite late, and venues still have rules such as no music after 10 p.m. You might also need to look into what your venue includes or allows for setup and breakdown times for your vendors.

When contracting at a venue, you might need to decide the start time of your wedding right then, or some give you flexibility to decide later on. The latest you want to confirm is when you start designing your invitations, because they'll need to include the start time. Think about when other key moments of the wedding will actually be taking place as well, such as when dinner is served, and make sure they feel okay to you. It's your wedding; have it when you want. But do think about your guest experience. You might like a disco nap before beginning your night out with an eleven o'clock happy hour, but your mom might have to be in her flats by then.

These specific timing details should be noted on the tab in the workbook called Run of Show. This will eventually be your minute-to-minute schedule for the entire event. Early in the planning, it can be vague and simply note things like ceremony start time or when an event must conclude. Here's an example of what a preliminary Run of Show can be:

TIME	ACTION
FRIDAY	
10:00 AM	Deliver Welcome Bags To Hotels
5:30 PM	Ceremony Rehearsal
6:00 PM	Rehearsal Dinner
8:30 PM	Welcome Party
SATURDAY	
5:00 PM	Invite
5:30 PM	Ceremony Start Time
6:00 PM	Cocktail Hour Begins
6:27 PM	Sunset
7:00 PM	Reception Begins
11:00 PM	Reception Ends
SUNDAY	
11:00 AM	Brunch Begins
2:00 PM	Brunch Ends

BOOKING THE THEATER

We'll focus on a more detailed version later. More important at this stage of planning are three important documents in our workbook that will help you determine the best place and time for your wedding:

1. **JMK Master Calendar**

   Our Master Calendar is meant to be malleable enough to work around you and your circumstances, and it lists just about everything you need to plan for. Some of the components might not be relevant to you or don't apply, in which case delete them. If you're starting the process with less than nine months to go, you might have a little bit of catch-up to do, but go for it! I've planned weddings on every timeline imaginable. Believe me, it's possible.

2. **Venue Options Worksheet**

   Populate this with all the places you're considering until you finally move forward with one.

3. **Vendor Contact Worksheet**

   Once you book your venue, it can be the first one you add to your Vendor Contact Sheet. As we move into the next chapters, be sure to keep this sheet updated whenever you confirm the next member of your dream team. Fill out all necessary fields to keep yourself organized, including contact information, social handles, and payment due dates.

Now that you've dreamed up the big picture, organized your priorities, determined your budget with your producers, and booked the theater for the show you've written, do you feel excited to move away from the spreadsheet for a moment and put your creative wedding cap on? The next chapter is one of my favorite elements of wedding planning, so I'm hoping your answer was a nice and loud, "We do!"

WE DO

MASTER CALENDAR

9–12+ Months Before	Notes
Purchase Your Copy of We Do	
Secure Venue & Date	
Draw Up Preliminary Guest Lists	
Determine Budget	
Research Hotels for Out-of-Town Guests	
Research Photographers	
Overall Vision Brainstorm, Including Design & Wedding Colors	
Browse Save The Dates & Invitation Options	
Shop for Wedding Dress	
Insure Engagement Ring	
8 Months Before	**Notes**
Buy Wedding Dress	
Shop for and Buy Veil	
Determine Wedding Officiant	
Secure Photographer	
Have an Engagement Photoshoot with Photographer	
Research Entertainment Options	
Book Entertainment	
Assess Major Venue Add-Ons (Lighting, etc)	
Determine Wedding Party	
Confirm Hotel Block	
Update Guest List and Collect Addresses	
Determine Hashtag	
Set Up Basic Wedding Website	
Order and Send Save the Dates	
Research Florist	
Save Flower Photos	

CONTINUED →

BOOKING THE THEATER

7 Months Before	Notes
Research and Book Caterer, if Venue Does Not Provide	
Research and Book Rehearsal Dinner & Brunch Options	
Book Florist	
Decide on bouquets, centerpieces, ceremony flowers, etc	
Book Videographer	
Set up Registry	
Book Cake Baker, If Needed	
6 Months Before	**Notes**
Confirm Additional AV needs	
Determine Fashion Look for Wedding Party	
Buy Bridesmaid Dresses	
Decide if Honeymoon Will Follow Wedding. If So, Begin Researching Options	
Book Ceremony/Cocktail Hour Musicians, If Needed	
5 Months Before	**Notes**
Start Shopping for Groomswear	
Shop for Wedding Shoes	
Work On Wedding Invitation Design	
Finalize Guest List	
Source Wedding Add-Ons (cake, photo booth, etc)	
Book Honeymoon	
Pick Out Wedding Bands	
Begin Planning Bachelor/Bachelorette Parties	
4 Months Before	**Notes**
Schedule Tastings	
Research Hair/Make-Up Artists, If Using	
Book Hair/Make-Up Artists	

CONTINUED →

MASTER CALENDAR

WE DO

MASTER CALENDAR

Review Invitation Proofs and Have Them Printed	
Arrange for Envelopes to be Printed With Addresses	
Discuss Transportation	
Complete Outfits with Accessories	
Weigh Sample Invitation to Determine Postage	
Design Meeting with Florist	
Begin Rental or Purchase Process for Groomsmen Suiting	
Decide On and Buy Accessories for Wedding Party	
Begin Planning Shower	
3 Months Before	**Notes**
Send invitations with RSVP system	
Plan Ceremony	
Plan Menu	
Source any Additional Design Elements	
Discuss Music Selections and Do-Not-Play List	
Source and Order Take-Home Favors	
Research Guidelines for Newspaper Announcement, if Interested	
2 Months Before	**Notes**
Have Final Fittings	
Finalize Orders for any Additional Items (Linens, Photo Booth, Lighting, Branded Items, etc)	
Begin Writing Vows	
Update Registry	
Have Food Tastings, Solidify Menu	
Meet with Entertainment	
Have Bachelor/Bachelorette Parties & Wedding Shower	
Send Invites for Rehearsal Dinner & Brunch	
Discuss Additional Signage	

CONTINUED →

BOOKING THE THEATER

1 Month Before	Notes
Order Table Numbers, Escort Cards, Programs and Menus	
Order Additional Signage	
Finalize Honeymoon Plans	
Begin Seating Chart	
Plan Hotel Welcome Bags & Bathroom Basket Items	
Draft Welcome Letter for Bags	
Order Venue Accessories (Guest Book, Gift Card Basket, etc)	
Chase any Lingering RSVPs	
Invite "B" List Guests	
Review Final Changes with Florist	
Plan Thank You Gifts for Wedding Party & Parents	
Determine Wedding Ushers if Needed	
Review Rooming Block with Hotel	
Confirm your Look is Complete	
Have Fitting For Groomswear	
Confirm Guest Count	
Review Ceremony with Officiant	
Build Run-Of-Show Including Hair & Makeup Schedule	
Hair & Make-Up Trials	
Review Music Selection with DJ/Band	
Finalize Shot List for Photographer	
Prepare Toasts	
Month Of	**Notes**
Confirm Outfits for Other Weekend Events	
Print Escort Cards	
Make Sure Order of Events and Speeches are Clear with Wedding Party & Family	

CONTINUED →

WE DO

Determine Day of Assignments for Wedding Party	
Obtain Marriage License	
Final Walk Thru at Venue, Submit Final Numbers	
Review Final Invoices	
Review Weekend Schedule	
Have 2nd Fitting for Groomswear, if Needed	
One Week Out	**Notes**
Finalize Seating Arrangements	
Finalize Run of Show and Send to All Vendors	
Confirm Transportation	
Prepare Payments	
Practice Your Vows	
Arrange for Any Handouts (programs, napkins, favors) to Be at Venue	
Have Groomswear Pressed	
Haircuts and Mani/Pedis	
Day Before	**Notes**
Deliver Welcome Bags to Hotel	
Rehearse Ceremony	
Rehearsal Dinner	
The Big Day!	**Notes**
Enjoy Your Wedding Day!	
Day After	**Notes**
Brunch	

MASTER CALENDAR

Scan to download the workbook.

WE DO

VENUE OPTIONS

NAME	STATUS	NEIGHBOR-HOOD	MAX CAPACITY	SITE FEE	MINIMUM SPEND
Ozdust Ballroom	Proposal Received	Under-ground Oz	450	10K	N/A
Harmonia Gardens	Proposal Received	Midtown	250	N/A	75K
La Cage aux Folles	Contacted; Awaiting Reply	St. Tropez			

72

BOOKING THE THEATER

FOOD/BEV	ADDITIONAL FEES	STARTING SPEND FOR OUR GUEST COUNT	AVAILABLE DATES	NOTES	SITE VISIT NOTES
Must Use Caterer from Preferred List	AV, Security, Admin & Tax	$ 13,500	5/4	Is ADA accessible	Loved!
All Done in House	Admin, Tax & Grat	$ 90,000	5/4	No outdoor space	The staircase is beautiful but some guests might struggle to descend

VENUE OPTIONS

VENDOR CONTACTS

NAME	COMPANY	ROLE	PHONE	EMAIL	IG HANDLE	CONTRACT
Dorothy Zbornak	The Sarcastic Step	Venue Manager	(555) 696-6969	YourGirl@thestep.com	TheSarcasticStep	confirmed
Blanche Devereaux	Southern Beats	DJ	(555) 696-6969	BlancheisYounger@sb.com	SouthernBeats	confirmed
Rose Nylund	St. Olaf Snaps	Photographer	(555) 696-6969	Rose@SOSnaps.com	SOSnaps	pending
Sophia Patrillo	No Wrinkles Here	Hair & Make Up	(555) 696-6969	Mother@NWH.com	NoWrinkles	pending

WE DO

BOOKING THE THEATER

NAME	TOTAL DUE	DEPOSIT $	DEPOSIT DATE	2ND DEPOSIT $	2ND DEPOSIT DATE	FINAL PAYMENT $	FINAL PAYMENT DATE	DAY OF (TIPS?)
Dorothy Zbornak	$100,000.00	$25,000.00	5/4	$25,000.00		$ 50,000.00	7/17	$ 3,000.00
Blanche Devereaux	$ 4,000.00	$ 1,000	5/4	N/A	N/A	$ 9,000.00	7/17	$ 250.00
Rose Nylund	$ 8,000.00	$ 4,000	5/10			$ 4,000.00	7/17	$ 250.00
Sophia Patrillo	$ 3,000.00	N/A				$ 3,000.00	7/17	20%

VENDOR CONTACTS

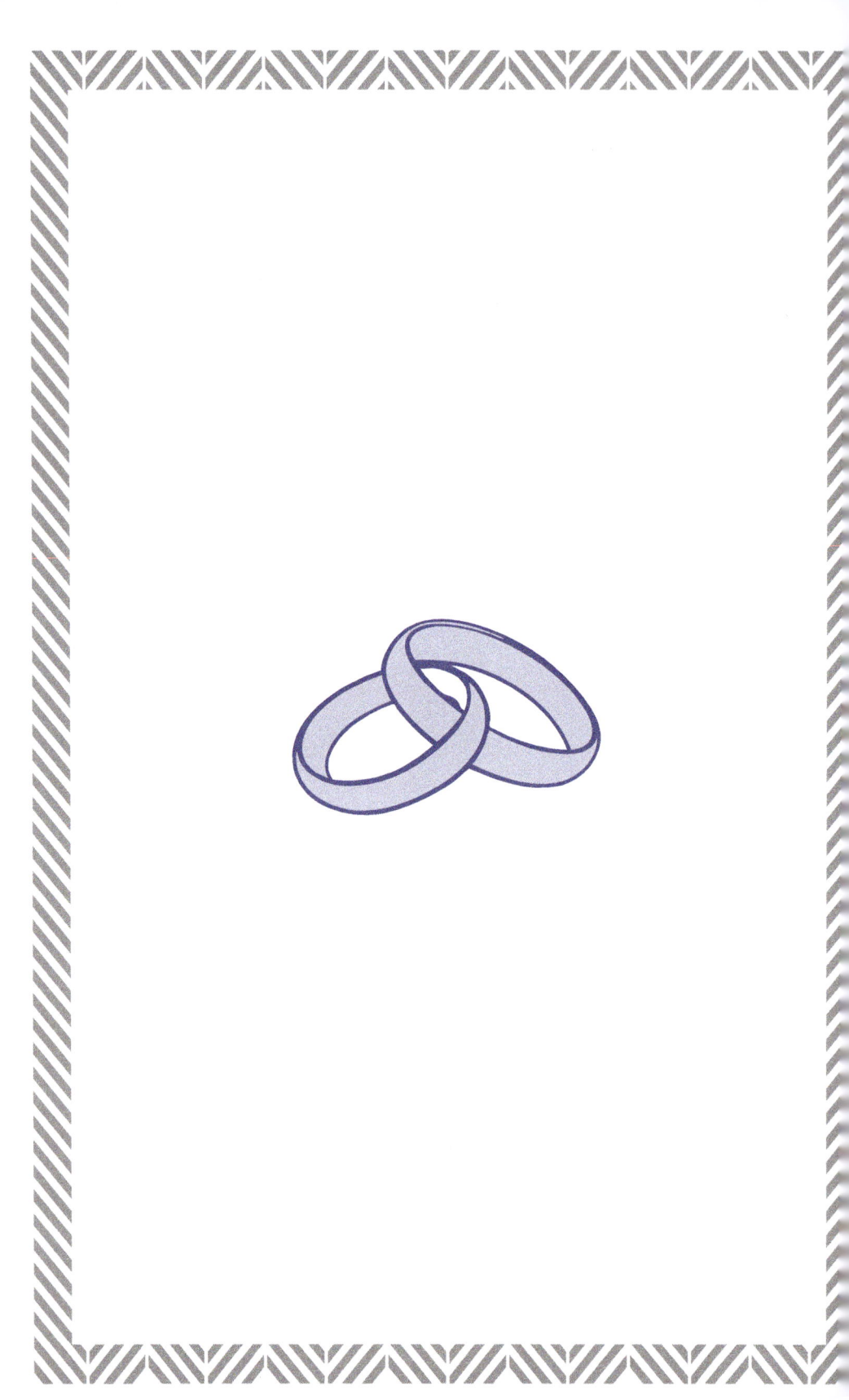

Chapter 4

THE DIRECTOR'S TOUCH

In the 1964 musical *Fiddler on the Roof*, there's a song called "Tradition" that perfectly captures the meaning of the word with its mention of mothers preparing daughters for marrying whomever their fathers choose for them. Thankfully that song likely doesn't relate to you, as you've picked your own person to marry regardless of the sewing skills you may have learned from your mom. And here in our little village of nontraditional weddings, you might say every one of us is a couple trying to plan their affair without breaking our necks—or playing the fiddle. So how do we keep our balance? There's one word that does *not* answer this question: tradition!

You've already made it to the fourth chapter, identifying as a couple who don't feel a traditional wedding is for you. But what does that really mean? Will you execute your wedding in such a way that no one will even recognize it as such an event? Probably not. But two of my favorite things to create with couples are both new traditions and reinvented ones. That's not to say I'm adverse to standard ones; sometimes tried and true is fitting. Our work here, though, is to find what fits for the two of *you*. And it's time for you to sit in the director's chair. It's these special touches that not only help tell your story but make the wedding exclusively yours.

Now, if you've already done your homework and read through the timeline we discussed in chapter 3, you'll notice that some of the topics in this chapter aren't necessarily top priority immediately after you book a venue. Depending on when your wedding date is, it might make sense to skip ahead for now and work on booking your photographer or designing your save the dates. But I do think beginning to wrap your head around this creative direction will inform some of the future practical decisions you'll have to make. As I've mentioned, wedding planning requires a lot of multitasking!

Before we can reinvent a tradition or spin one on its axis, it's important for you to know where some traditions originate. As you can probably imagine, many are very gendered and heteronormative. Some of the following facts might be interesting to you, entertaining, or honestly a bit puzzling. In some Chinese cultures, for instance, a best man is supposed to be unmarried, and a groom chooses someone less close to him as long as that person's status is single. Can you even?

The first section assumes there's a bride and groom who'll be marrying, and I realize many of you might not fit into that breakdown or identify with the titles. If this is you, just have fun as we go back in time and learn about how these things used to break down. As you read, you'll find many JMK Tips. Take notes about what's speaking to you, what isn't, and ways you can make each component your own.

THE CAST LIST

- **THE COUPLE**
  - **The Groom**
    A groom is a male who has found the woman he wants to marry and proposed to her. Traditionally he first asks her parents for permission, then he proposes to her with a ring.

- **The Bride**

    A bride is a female who has said yes to a proposal. All the planning is centered around creating the vision for her wedding day. During the ceremony, she's given away by her father or both parents.

■ THE PARTY

By "the party," I'm not referring to the reception here. In most weddings, there's what's known as a bridal or (less gendered) wedding party. It can consist of all or some of the following:

- **Bridesmaids**

    The bride selects her closest girlfriends and family members to be a part of her entourage. They support the maid of honor and assist with all planning responsibilities along the way, including showers and bachelorette parties. They also take on different hosting responsibilities during the wedding so that the bride doesn't have to worry about anything.

- **Groomsmen**

    The entourage the groom selects consists of groomsmen, and there's the same quantity as bridesmaids. Their main duty is organizing the bachelor party. At the wedding they usually escort the bridesmaids down the aisle and sometimes help seat guests if there are no ushers.

- **Maid or Matron of Honor**

    The person the bride selects as her number one go-to-for-everything assistant is the maid or matron of honor, usually the bride's best friend or sister. She helps the bride through the entire process, constantly serving as an extra set of hands and eyes.

She organizes the shower with the bridesmaids, is closest to the bride while getting ready, and is there for constant emotional support. Usually she toasts the couple during the reception, and she's the last bridesmaid to walk down the aisle, carrying the groom's wedding band until the ring exchange.

- **Best Man**
  The groom selects a best man to be his personal aide and consultant through all stages of wedding planning, usually the groom's best friend, brother, or any other male figure he feels closest to. While in many ways this is the male counterpart to the maid or matron of honor, traditionally the latter is much more involved in all aspects of the bride's plans. The duties of a best man can include planning a bachelor party, consulting on fashion for the groom, organizing the other groomsmen, getting the groom to the ceremony on time, and giving a memorable toast. He also often holds the bride's wedding band until the ring exchange.

- **Father of the Bride**
  The biggest tradition associated with the role of father of the bride—besides mimicking Steve Martin's iconic character—is paying for the whole thing. Therefore, other money-related duties usually fall on him as well, such as paying vendors the night of and making sure everyone who needs to be tipped is looked after.

- **Father of the Groom**
  When the tradition of the father of the bride paying for the whole wedding is being met, usually the father of the groom pays for the rehearsal dinner.

Essentially, they get a financial break with this event for having a male child!

- **Mother of the Bride**
  The nature of the role of mother of the bride should be up to the bride, but a domineering mother might see it otherwise. Her duties can include being the wedding planner and guest-list moderator, attending or hosting the bridal shower, and being a voice of reason during the whole process.

- **Mother of the Groom**
  Usually the mother of the groom throws the rehearsal dinner with the father of the groom; other than that, she doesn't have many official duties other than to participate in the mother–son dance, wear something generic, and keep her mouth shut!

- **Officiant**
  The officiant is whoever performs the marriage ceremony. It can be a priest, rabbi, justice of the peace, city official, or anyone else who can perform weddings, and they're usually the first person to walk down the aisle.

- **Flower Girl**
  The flower girl is usually a relative's or friend's child who's less than ten years old. She walks down the aisle scattering petals before the bride, and after her hopefully adorable stroll, she usually sits with her parents.

- **Ring Bearer**
  The ring bearer is the male counterpart to the flower girl and is usually a young boy of similar age.

He walks down the aisle just before her with a pillow holding symbolic rings.

- **Juniors**
  When couples want to include any youngsters in their wedding party, those youngsters are referred to as junior groomsmen and junior bridesmaids. They can be dressed similarly to their senior versions, and they participate in everything they're allowed to or are capable of, sans the X-rated bachelor activities.

- **Ushers**
  Ushers are male or female persons of honor who are in charge of seating the guests for the ceremony.

JMK TIPS

Reinvent These Titles!

Titles are such a wonderful place to get creative. As a male feminist, I've never thought it was fair that our gender is "the best" while the female counterpart was a "maid" or "matron." May the best woman win! Among many others, we've seen "bridesmen," "groomsgirls," "best boys," "best people," "our squad," "our peeps," "flower boys," "lords of the rings," "chosen family," and "our divas." People who are close to you won't care what their actual title is, especially if you've anointed them with something more personal.

Don't Get Stuck on Symmetry

It's not crucial to have the same number of people on both sides or to make each side one gender. Many couples have friends with whom they're both equally close. Celebrate the nuanced circle you're a part of!

See It Through Their Eyes

Many nontraditional JMK couples have expressed not wanting a party of any kind. If you feel the same, take a moment to think about the people who would be included if you were having one. It's an incredible honor when someone asks you to be a part of their wedding, so why not honor the friends and family members who are important to you? You do you, just make sure you consider it from all sides.

Size Doesn't Matter

Deciding who makes the cut should not keep you up at night. Sure, there might be more of a logistic challenge for a larger group to go on a bachelor weekend or for figuring out how to get everyone down the aisle. But these are challenges you can find solutions for. Include who your heart is telling you to.

Honor Elsewhere

There are other ways to honor those who are special to you but who you don't ask to be in your wedding party. You can ask them to perform a reading in the ceremony, be a witness to the signing of the marriage license, or even be the presenter of something, such as the vows to be acknowledged during the ceremony.

THE SCRIPT

■ THE CEREMONY

Do not undervalue or underestimate the ceremony component of your wedding. Tons of JMK couples have expressed something along the lines of, "We just want to keep it short and sweet." Those adjectives aren't necessarily bad for a ceremony, but they're impersonal and generic. A ceremony does not have to be long or include a history lesson to enable guests to think, feel, and reflect, and the reception that follows is in celebration of that ceremony. Allowing this part of the wedding to be one that takes guests to an elevated emotional state is part of the recipe for a memorable event. To achieve that, it's important to make your guests feel engaged and included.

Just as with everything else, I absolutely adore giving a ceremony a new spin, tradition, or time when it happens. I once had a couple tell me they disliked that the exchange of vows was too early in the programming of the night, so we broke up their entire wedding into three acts and put the reception and other elements in between. They exchanged vows at the "eleven o'clock number," a theater term meaning the most heightened moment toward the end of a show, and after they were pronounced as "married," we served dessert.

Before we dive deeper into nontraditional wedding components, let's evaluate the opposite. The traditional order for a wedding ceremony is this:

1. **Processional**

   The ceremony begins with selected music as the entire wedding party walks down the aisle. Different cultures and religions vary how the bride and groom come down

THE DIRECTOR'S TOUCH

the aisle. Sometimes both parents walk on either side, while other times only the father walks the bride. The processional usually goes in this order:

a. Officiant
b. Grandparents of the groom
c. Grandparents of the bride
d. Pairs of bridesmaids and groomsmen
e. The maid or matron of honor and the best man
f. The ring bearer and the flower girl
g. The groom's parents and the groom
h. The bride's parents and the bride

Keep in mind that some weddings don't involve the groom or groomsmen walking down the aisle; they simply get into place before the procession begins. Because I'm a planner who works to make weddings feel like they're about a couple rather than one person, you can probably imagine where I stand on this!

JMK TIPS

It's All About You Two!

Start with how the two of you will be entering, and work backward from there. Try to picture what you want to feel in that moment. You can still be escorted by parents (or honorary ones) without it implying they're giving you away. Does that feel right to you? The two of you can also enter individually, whether it's one after the next or at the same time. An aisle can also be designed with two entrances.

Place Your Wedding Party

There is no wedding rule written anywhere saying that a wedding party must stand on either side of the couple after walking down the aisle. In fact, if you've ever had to do this, you probably understand that standing to the side of the main event can be a less-than-ideal feeling. You can always arrange to have reserved seating waiting for them in the first rows.

Consider Guest Seating

Traditionally, weddings have had a bride's side and a groom's side where respective guests sit. Very few couples still deem this important, but do think about close family, the wedding party if they're not with you, and any other VIPs you may want to reserve seating for. Ideally, they should be seated on the side opposite the person they're connected to who's marrying because that way they can spend the ceremony with a view of their face rather than their butt.

2. **Opening Remarks & Ceremony Rituals**

   There are so many different components to wedding ceremonies, from the aisle march to the vows. They vary by culture, religion, and a slew of other factors, but they usually include opening remarks by the officiant. What follows might be a blessing, prayer, reading, passing of the rings, candle lighting, song, or explanation of customs, and there's sometimes drinking of wine, circling of each other, smoking of tobacco, grabbing of shoes . . . the list goes on.

JMK TIPS

Incorporate a Fun Part of Your Story
One JMK couple had their two best friends read the text exchange they both had with the couple after the couple came home from their first date. Another JMK couple celebrated that they met at a nightlife establishment and did two shots of tequila as a riff on a wine blessing.

Avoid Meaningless Additions
A reading is worth being read or a song is worth being sung only if you have some type of connection to it.

Remind Guests of the Uniqueness of the Moment
Having done so many weddings for the LGBTQ+ community, I think it's important to remind guests that this hasn't always been an option for our community and that it isn't a right granted all around the world.

3. **Vows & Exchange of Rings**
   Vows are promises each partner makes to the other after (or while) exchanging rings. Certain religious traditions involve saying standard vows, while in other cultures and in our more modern times, couples write their own. I strongly encourage you to write your own vows. It's one of the best ways to ensure a ceremony is from the heart, which is the most important thing. You and your fiancé can write these together or surprise each other, just make sure you're both on the same page about length and tone. If during this part of the ceremony your

officiant will be prompting you with any questions along the lines of "Do you take" or "Do you promise," be sure the rest of what's said is something you want to answer affirmatively. We live in modern times, and you're not obligated to promise monogamy if it isn't something you practice. Are you stumped on where to begin? Check out the Vow Writing tab in the workbook. There's also a sample at the end of this chapter.

Another opportunity to engage your guests here is to really make your vows part of this moment. Just as you're about to make promises to one another, your guests can make a promise to you. The officiant can state something along the lines of, "Before our couple says their I do's, I have a question for all you, their closest friends and family: Do you promise to support them as they enter marriage, to be there for them through the ups and downs they may encounter, and to encourage their relationship to flourish?" Of course your officiant should use this as a starting point and make the text their own, but it should lead to your crowd unanimously answering with the title of this book.

JMK TIP

Many religious and cultural practices incorporated into weddings are rooted in outdated traditions. I've planned many Jewish weddings in my career, so I know that if you're going to sign a ketubah (a Jewish marriage certificate) beforehand, you need to read through the text included when selecting a design you like. Ketubahs were initially designed to protect the bride and obligate the groom to look after her welfare. Now you can find ones that specialize in equality for any gender. Jewish ceremonies also

> typically conclude with the groom stomping on a glass. I've done plenty of weddings with two glasses for two grooms as well as for progressive brides who wanted the same experience. Explore the ceremony traditions of your culture and see whether they work for the story you're telling. You both might want to jump the broom!

4. **Pronouncement, Kiss & Recessional**

    After the vows and exchange of rings, a couple is officially announced as married and kisses. Then the music starts, and the couple walks back down the aisle, which is called the recessional. The wedding party follows the couple in the reverse order they entered, so the officiant is the last person to exit.

JMK TIP

Final Words Matter!

The traditional last sentences of a pronouncement are, "I now pronounce you man and wife. You may kiss the bride." Chances are that's not how you want this main event to end. Think about what you want to hear, such as

> "Partners in life,"
> "Equally wed,"
> "Legally married,"
> "Husbands,"
> "Brides," or
> "People who need people,"

then conclude with "You may kiss each other" or "And now, make out!"

As I mentioned earlier, these are not decisions you have to hone in on at the initial stage of planning, but you'll want to revisit this chapter when you're ready to focus on more of these details. And don't forget this book's appendix if you're looking for information on religious traditions.

As you do design your ceremony, whether it be beautifully epic or short and sweet, I encourage you to have a rehearsal. This traditionally takes place the day before, preceding the rehearsal dinner. While some couples tell me they prefer to hold their rehearsal in the space where the wedding will take place, squeezing it in on the day of the wedding can be very challenging, and venues rarely hold rehearsals in the wedding space the day before. Instead on the day before your wedding, assemble everyone who's involved in your ceremony and just do what's known in theater as a "cue to cue": Discuss the order of people walking in, where they go after, who has the rings, what side the microphone is on for a reading, and what the cue is for each person's exit. It's fine if you can't arrange for this in your actual ceremony venue; a makeshift aisle and an altar will suffice.

■ Time Alone

Enjoying some time alone is a tradition that varies culturally, but it allows couples some alone time right after the wedding ceremony before they greet their guests. In Judaism it's called the *cheder yichud*, or "room of seclusion," which supposedly strengthens the marriage bond. Whatever the culture or reason, I encourage all couples to take this opportunity to not only savor the sanctity of what has just become official but also have a bite to eat and something to drink.

THE DIRECTOR'S TOUCH

JMK TIP

When I escort my JMK couples to the room for time alone, we usually joke about how now's the time to consummate the marriage (emphasis on the word *joke*). I'm not saying don't be affectionate, but you've spent all day getting ready to look your best and still have a reception to get to.

■ RECEIVING LINE

Traditionally, a receiving line involves the parents of the couple, though sometimes the wedding party joins them, and even the newlyweds might too . . . if they aren't taking time to themselves. Technically, for it to be a reception, guests must be received. En route to the cocktail hour, the hosts exchange hugs, kisses, handshakes, and general wishes of congratulations.

JMK TIP

While the idea of a receiving line is beautiful in principle, it's a wedding planner's nightmare because it always causes a logistical bottleneck. I think they're helpful only if the ceremony and reception are in separate places and you're trying to kill time in between. Otherwise, it's best to let guests get to the food and drink, and they can make their way more organically to all the hosts they want to congratulate.

■ THE RECEPTION

The reception is a party to celebrate the whole occasion. Receptions range in tone and style; some are wild dance parties, while others are formal and restrained dining experiences. We'll discuss food, beverages, and entertainment later, as they're a tradition important to all weddings, but for now here's the general breakdown of a wedding reception:

- **Cocktail Hour**

Cocktail hour usually immediately follows the ceremony, and it allows guests a chance to have a cocktail and mingle before heading into the reception space. However, I've done plenty of weddings for which the cocktail hour was before the ceremony. Either way, it's a great opportunity for guests to visit with one another before a more structured dining experience later. At some point during the cocktail hour, guests might begin to find their table place cards at an escort table. The couple will usually join cocktail hour after they've finished their time alone. Sometimes this hour is also needed for logistics, such as needing to flip the main space from ceremony to reception.

JMK TIP

Plan to complete any posed and group photos *before* the event begins. That way you can spend cocktail hour doing whatever you'd like!

- **Introduction**

Once the guests have entered the reception area, a bandleader or DJ will make an introduction. This might include the wedding party and parents, or sometimes it's just the couple. The announcement usually goes something like, "Please welcome to the dance floor for the first time, Mr. and Mrs. Smith!" The newly married couple then enters while their guests cheer in celebration of the couple's new status.

JMK TIP

Introductions can be fun if they're done with a nod and a wink, especially if you're opening the reception with a party vibe. Create a funny sentence for each member of the wedding party and let this be the first time they hear it as a surprise. If that's not your jam, it's perfectly fine for only the couple to be announced. Just like the pronouncement, really consider the words here. Chances are you're not Mr. and Mrs. Smith! Think about what you're really celebrating and consider a phrase like, "for the first time as legally married!" Also, if you're like many JMK couples and don't want any more attention at this time, it's perfectly fine to go without a formal announcement. You do you!

- **First Dance**

After a couple has been introduced, they usually share in a first dance for all the guests to watch. Some couples go to great measures to prepare for this moment by taking dance lessons.

JMK TIP

Be authentic. If the two of you dancing in front of everyone isn't your style, you'll still be married, and if milking this moment with a custom mash-up that turns into a flash mob is you, then go for it.

- **Father–Daughter & Mother–Son Dances**

Family member dances usually happen later in the night. The bride dances with her father, and later the groom is asked to join along with his mother. Sometimes they're followed by all the parent–child pairs at the reception.

JMK TIP

Celebrate this family moment if that feels right. So many JMK couples over the years have loved this tradition, while for others it can be triggering if someone is no longer with them or is unsupportive. Also, be creative with your song choice. You can be sentimental, funny, or ironic, or you can combine this into one moment known as a whole-family dance.

- **Bouquet Toss**

The once single bride is now married, and it's time to pass the torch with a bouquet toss. All the single girls line up, and the bride faces away from them and tosses her bouquet into the air for one of the girls to catch. Whoever does is supposed to have good luck in being the next to meet Mr. Right.

JMK TIP

Be ironic. These really dated traditions can be fun if you put your spin on them.

- **Garter Toss**

The tradition of tossing a garter involves the bride wearing one underneath her dress. After the bouquet toss, the groom removes the garter from the bride, then throws it into the air for all the eligible bachelors. The same superstition about the bouquet toss applies to their romantic luck.

JMK TIP

When I was eight years old, I caught the garter at my aunt and uncle's wedding, but I did not meet the girl of my dreams shortly thereafter, or ever for that matter. This practice is rarely done in earnest anymore, which is how I think it should be done. However, if you want to make some fun of this moment, go for it. If it's authentic, take that harness of your betrothed and throw it to the crowd. Let's see what that portends!

- **Cake Cutting**

Serving wedding cake is ubiquitous to a traditional wedding, but it must be cut first, and this is usually done by the bride and groom in full view of all guests. Sometimes after slicing they feed each other a bite. The rest of the cake is then sliced by the staff and served to all the guests.

JMK TIP

Feel free to skip this if cake isn't your thing. And if you are having a wedding cake, you can opt to cut it in front of your guests or more privately. Either way, if you're feeding each other, keep it civilized. No need for a cake to be thrown in the face of the person you've just married!

- **Last Dance**

When the night is just about to conclude, the band or DJ announces that it's the last dance for all guests. Couples preselect a meaningful song for this moment, most picking something all guests can participate in.

Once you have a general sense of which (if any) of these elements you want to include, add them to your Run of Show. Later you'll want to discuss this with those who'll be in charge of food service and music, as having the timing in harmony is key.

Gift Registries

Registering for gifts is an age-old tradition that allows a couple to communicate to their guests what they'd like as presents. It might sound assuming to you, but it's still expected with weddings. Even if you truly don't want gifts at all, people will still bring them, so at least it's better to have a little control. Trust me. Any client in the past who has pushed back on this has ended up with random gifts.

The old days of picking one place like Bloomingdales and going around with a scan gun are gone. But companies such as Zola have enabled registries to be a combination of physical items from different stores, ways guests can treat you to experiences on your honeymoon, and opportunities to raise money for causes that are important to you. The best part is that you can return anything you later change your mind about. It's proper wedding etiquette to keep a registry open for up to a year after a wedding because that's considered reasonable timing for sending gifts.

JMK TIP

You're hosting a wedding. Don't feel shy about letting people give you something to say congratulations.

- **OTHER EVENTS**
  - **Rehearsal Dinner**

  Following the rehearsal of the next day's ceremony, a rehearsal dinner kicks off the weekend's festivities. The etiquette is to invite all out-of-town guests, family, and members of the wedding party. Activities usually include roasting the couple. The dinner also gives the bride and groom a chance to thank everyone who has helped plan the wedding.

JMK TIP

Don't let this turn into a second wedding! And there's really no rule book stating that everyone who falls into one of these categories must be served a plated dinner. If this group of invitees is large, you can have more of a cocktail-style welcome party. You should still serve some food, but advertise it as "drinks and bites" so that guests don't expect dinner.

  - **Farewell Brunch**

  A farewell brunch is the grand finale to the whole weekend experience. Usually, the same guests from the rehearsal dinner are invited, and it's the last opportunity for all guests to congratulate the couple and their families before heading home.

>
> **JMK TIP**
>
> Do you loathe going to these brunches when you attend a wedding? Many JMK couples have and simply didn't want to throw one. You can send guests home from the wedding with your neighborhood's best bagel or pastry and let them enjoy it in the morning. In the mood to host something other than a brunch? Keep the party going with more of an afternoon party. The guests that go for it will appreciate not having the earlier call time of brunch. You can also host something super casual in your suite, telling guests to stop by for coffee, a pastry, and a hug goodbye.

Now that you've explored the areas in need of personalization, you can view three tabs you'll be revisiting and filling in as you go, jotting down your notes and ideas as these concepts evolve with you:

- Ceremony Brainstorm
- Wedding Party List
- Vow-Writing Exercise

Here's a sample of each one:

THE DIRECTOR'S TOUCH

ELEMENTS	WANT	DO NOT WANT
CULTURAL	Passing of the Rings	Bagpipes
RELIGIOUS	Chuppah, Kiddush, Break the Glass	Seven Blessings
TRADITIONAL	Moment of Silence	Unity Candle
MODERN	Group Vows, Everyone to have a Drink	Group Sing A Long
MUSICAL	A song by Alysha	Strings
OTHER	Reading about Same Sex Marriage	Any other readings

CEREMONY BRAINSTORM

WE DO

WEDDING PARTY LIST

PERSON 1		MUTUAL	PERSON 2	
TITLES	NAME		TITLES	NAME
Groom		☐	Brideish	
Best Man		☐	Maid of Fabulousness	
Groomsman		☐	Bridesmaid	
Groomsman		☐	Bridesman	
Mother		☐	Mother	
Father		☐	Father	
Siblings		☐	Siblings	
Steps		☐	Steps	
Ring Bearer		☐	Ring Bearer	
Flower Child		☐	Flower Child	
Officiant		☐	Officiant	
Witness		☐	Witness	
Witness		☐	Witness	
Usher		☐	Usher	
Usher		☐	Usher	
Dog Escort		☐	Dog Escort	
Other		☐	Other	

THE DIRECTOR'S TOUCH

_____, you are my
(partner's name)

_____,
(what you call them)

my _____ and my
(another loving noun)

_____.
(nickname you use)

Every day my feelings of

_____
(some of your feelings towards them)

grow stronger. I couldn't imagine my life without you, or being anywhere else right now besides declaring them in front of

_____
(a description of your guests)

right here _____.
(wedding location)

VOW-WRITING EXERCISE

WE DO

WHAT DID YOU KNOW?
WAS IT SOMETHING RIGHT AT FIRST OR GRADUAL?
EXPAND ON THAT.

When we met at _____,
(the place)

I knew _____.
(what your first felt)

HOW DID YOUR CLOSEST FRIENDS OR RELATIVES REACT
WHEN THEY FIRST MET THEM? WAS THIS IMPORTANT TO YOU?

My _____ response
(first person you told)'s

was _____
(their reaction)

and I knew they were

_____.
(how you felt)

HOW HAVE YOU CHANGED? WHAT'S IMPROVED IN YOUR LIFE SINCE BEING
TOGETHER? WHAT WOULD YOU HAVE NEVER DONE ON YOUR OWN? THINK
ABOUT LITTLE, DAY-TO-DAY THINGS AND ALSO MAJOR, BIG DIFFERENCES.

Before I met you, I _____,
(describe previous behavior)

and now I _____.
(descrive how you've changed)

VOW-WRITING EXERCISE

THE DIRECTOR'S TOUCH

THIS CAN BE SERIOUS, FUNNY OR BOTH.

We share a mutual love for _____, but we balance
(things you have in common)
each other out because I prefer _____ to your choice
(something very you)
of _____, and we make
(something very them)
that work.

WHAT DO YOU MISS MOST WHEN THEY ARE AWAY?

When you're not around I _____, and then
(how you feel when apart)
when we're back together it's like _____.
(how you feel upon return)

VOW-WRITING EXERCISE

WE DO

WAS THERE AN "A-HA" MOMENT BETWEEN THE TWO OF YOU? DID THEY DO SOMETHING WHERE YOU KNEW THEY WERE YOUR SPECIAL PERSON?

You have many special qualities, like _____,
(unique features about them)
but when you did _____, that's
(something big)
when I _____.
(evoked in you)

WHAT HAVE YOU LEARNED FROM THEM? WHAT DO YOU THINK THAT BROUGHT OUT IN YOU? WHAT DO YOU BRING TO THE TABLE AS PARTNERS?

Your _____ has
(skill they have)
taught me _____
(something you've learned)
and shown me that together we _____.
(strength as a couple)

VOW-WRITING EXERCISE

THE DIRECTOR'S TOUCH

WAS THERE AN EXPERIENCE YOU SHARED THAT WAS A BODING MOMENT, EVEN IF NOT A PARTICULARLY ROMANTIC ONE?

When we _____,
            (experience shared)
although at the time I thought

_____, then
        (your first feelings)
I realized _____.
                  (where you landed)

WHAT DO YOU WANT TO DECLARE IN FRONT OF EVERYONE?

And so, today in front of

_____
        (description of guests)
I would like to promise you this

                (what you vow to do in the relationship)

VOW-WRITING EXERCISE

WE DO

WHAT PART OF YOUR LIFE AHEAD TOGETHER
ARE YOU MOST EXCITED ABOUT?

With you by my side, I look forward to

(future dreams)

WHAT IS THE MOST PERSONAL WAY YOU EXPRESS YOUR LOVE?

And I love you with all my

(where your feelings emanate from)

VOW-WRITING EXERCISE

THE DIRECTOR'S TOUCH

The first two you can work on together, but for the third I recommend you both complete a copy individually. Whether you end up sharing them with each other is up to you. Answer everything knowing you won't use it all at your actual wedding; this is just a way to get started, and you can write as much or as little as you want in response to the questions. If you're confused how your answers might get worded into vows, for instance, below each question is a sample sentence that allows you to fill in the blanks. Once you've completed those, string them together and change my words to your own. You're creating heartfelt vows, not wedding *Mad Libs*! Reread them to check whether you're repeating similar thoughts or sentiments, and edit accordingly.

Some of the shows that have had the most impact are those for which the director's touch made it leap off the stage and become an experience I couldn't stop thinking about. Do you feel ready to make your wedding that kind of one-night-only experience? If so, let's get the audience into their seats!

Chapter 5

ADVERTISING YOUR SHOW

"Extra! Extra! Hey, look at the headlines! Historical news is being made!"

Okay, so maybe this isn't the biggest scoop of the decade. Or maybe it is. Either way, if you want anyone to attend your show, you have to let them know about it. This is one of the areas of wedding planning that has evolved tremendously since I started my career. No, I'm not old enough to insinuate that I was working when invitations arrived by horse and buggy, but both the advancement of the digital era and the green movement have shifted just how much paper is produced. There are also margins of error in physical items getting lost in the mail, and digital items often wind up in people's junk mail or simply go unnoticed in this society of constantly being emailed.

If I've already confused you, I'm sorry. Like everything else in wedding planning, there's no right or wrong way, there's simply your way. Whichever way you choose, it's important to know that invitations set the tone for what's to follow. If your dream is to keep everything simple and low-key, there's no need for a lot of fuss with invitations. But if you're letting everyone know to prepare for the event of the century, this is where all the fun begins. For the sake of my theater analogies, think of this like building the buzz for an opening. Save the dates are like the announcement after a theater has been secured and casting is set, and invitations are like when the marquee goes up. The programs, place cards, table numbers, menus, and favor notes are like the playbill and merch that are displayed, and the thank-you cards are like messages sent from the theater company to the audience letting them know the theater is grateful for their support.

You'll want to get the tone right for the announcement of your show. As you walk through the process of creating your save the dates and invitations, really think about what it will be like for your guests to receive them and what impression you want to make. It's a fabulous opportunity to think creatively; there's no need for an ivory envelope with old-fashioned calligraphy unless that's truly your style.

One thing I stress as we move ahead to design ideas is that all these materials should correlate in some way. That doesn't mean they have to be matchy-matchy, but they should be of similar tone and style. If you've selected wedding colors, that can be a helpful way to start, but it's not imperative. If something like a vintage postcard of the town you're getting married in feels like the right save the date, this doesn't mean those colors must be used in your flowers and table linens. In terms of the design process, and depending on the level of importance to you and your budget, you should assess whether you want to hire a designer or handle this on your own. Having a professional design these items can save you time and stress and give you something truly custom, but it will also cost more. If hiring a designer isn't in your budget, there are fantastic websites, such as Minted, Zola, and various stores on Etsy, that allow you to do some level of customization to their existing templates. You can usually order samples in advance and then see how your personalized text looks on them, and you can play with color and embellishments, such as embossing or foil pressing.

ADVERTISING YOUR SHOW

If this is starting to sound overwhelming already, I understand. It easily can be. Just one site can have thousands of invitations, and nobody should look at that many! This is where hiring a designer can be very advantageous. Besides producing the finished product, they can ask the right questions to hone in on your style. If you're going about this yourself, *you* must ask the questions and let your answers inform you. How can you best express the overall vision of your show? What types of fonts represent your wedding, something modern and hip, or something more classic? Words often used in figuring out the style include *art deco, bohemian, bold, botanical, classic, formal, funny, illustrative, maximalist, minimalist, modern, rustic,* or *vintage.* Do any of those descriptors feel right?

Some couples also like to have logos created. This could be a monogram of your initials, an image that has significance, or just a design that calls to you. If you opt for a logo, you can use it as much or as little as you like. It can be at the top of every printed item and designed into your cake, or it can be just a simple accent on your save the dates.

Once you feel like you have a sense of your style, start getting organized with the individual components, or what's known as your suite.

SAVE THE DATES

Again, don't think of the acronym for save the dates as some unwanted surprise after a rendezvous. This component is both a practical and important step of the planning process. It's customary to send them six to eight months before your wedding. I've had several clients in the past tell me they'd prefer to send them sooner, and sometimes they even want to do them immediately after they book a venue, fearing that people's calendars could book up. If you're in that camp and your wedding is almost a year out, and if you've already let your family and besties know, do not rush this process. The main reason the six- to eight-month timeframe works so well is because at about half a year away, you already have a good grasp on your guest list. And save the dates are not only a wonderful way to create your wedding buzz but also extremely helpful in gauging how many people will be attending. Even though guests aren't obligated to RSVP to save the dates, many will respond in some way, so you'll have a better handle on numbers. You might hear from your dad's cousin, "We loved the save the date, but we have a cruise booked that weekend," which might allow you to invite some of your "maybes" down the line.

There are two important rules to keep in mind when it comes to etiquette here: (1) If you send someone a save the date, you're obligated to invite them (unless you find out a really juicy story afterward that gives you permission to revoke the offer), and (2) you're always allowed to invite people who didn't receive a save the date. If you just can't decide about certain guests, it's best to skip the save the date and make a judgment call when it comes time for invitations.

Printing versus going digital is another element to consider. If you already know whether you're 100 percent "team printed" or 100 percent "team digital," you're ahead of the game. If you're torn or don't have the budget to print both components, do digital save the dates and print the invitations. Sending a digital save the date can also be a way to collect addresses for the invitations that will follow. If you're printing these, they're done similar to an invitation, as a singular item sent in an envelope. Even if you're designing something similar to a postcard, I recommend sending it in an envelope so that guests receive it in pristine condition.

As I mentioned, it's not necessary for the design of your save the dates to completely match that of your invitations. The most important thing is communicating the essential information. If you're finding yourself trying to strike a balance between silly and serious, your save the dates are where you can have fun, while your invitations can be more classic. I had a client who loved disco balls but was planning to have a classic black-tie wedding, so they felt disco balls were inappropriate on the invitations. But using them on the save the dates was fun and got everyone excited. Similarly, you can use a photograph of the two of you and add text. And this doesn't have to be a romantic or glamorous photo; if you're planning with a sense of humor, for instance, an unexpected photo might be the ticket. You could also incorporate something that's iconic or identifies the city or venue where the wedding will be taking place. A building's architecture, a city's skyline, or an activity associated with the region can all be places of inspiration.

Save the dates also aren't limited to being printed on card stock. You can send them as a magnet, a scroll, or even a packaged goodie. Whatever suits the two of you most when it comes to the information works, and I say less is more.

Regardless of what you choose, your save the dates should include the following:

- Your names
- The actual words "save the date"
- The date
- The location (just the city and state or international country, not the venue)
- The link for your wedding website (or a QR code that leads invitees to it)

The other practical perk of save the dates is that they do the tedious work of collecting addresses and correct spellings. Yes, those are important, even if you're sending someone a graphic of an envelope that opens on a screen. And you need to make a few decisions at this point. One is whether you want to use titles when addressing your envelopes. As you can probably imagine, many of the rules of etiquette are pretty old-school and don't always work for nontraditional weddings. Like why are doctors and judges the only professions entitled to a different title when, frankly, I'm quite proud of what I do for a living? And if you're inviting people who use different pronouns, this is important to get right. Many JMK couples opt to use just first and last names as the path of least resistance.

> **JMK TIP**
>
> Do you have a handful of guests who might be offended by receiving something without a title, while many others won't care? Do a mix! Your guests won't be opening their envelopes around each other.

Another element you must decide on here is your policy on guests, plus-ones, and children. If budget or venue capacity hasn't already determined this for you, let me share what's commonly accepted as appropriate. Traditionally, you let a guest bring a guest if they're a member of your wedding party, a close relative, or a friend of your significant other. It's also permissible if you're worried about a guest attending alone. This is another place where you don't have to follow the rules. From what I've witnessed (and encountered) of single guests at weddings, I know they're usually just fine going solo.

As for children, this has often been a place of contention for many JMK couples. There are many factors to consider as you make your rules here. You could simply say "no children" as a blanket rule to avoid any confusion, or you could invite only the children you actually know and have a relationship with. You might not care if there's a screaming child stealing focus from you, in which case please teach me your tricks. Most importantly, if you're allowing someone to invite a guest or bring their little ones, you should include that on both the save the dates and the invitations.

It's now time to revisit the workbook and review the worksheets from chapter 2. Flesh out your guest list, fine-tune your budget, and finalize any other additional information you need before getting to the invitations.

INVITATIONS

The preliminary information has been received by your guests, and now it's time for the graphic design element of your show: the invitations! These are usually more complex and contain more information than save the dates, and hopefully by this point you've completed the process of identifying your style. There are more fonts, colors, shapes, paperweights, and styles than could ever be listed in one place. But like many other aspects of wedding planning, the traditions of how wedding invitations are worded are a bit archaic. Let's start with the information they should include, and I'll explain from there:

- Your names
- Who's hosting or throwing the event (besides you)
- The date and time
- The location (both places if the ceremony and reception are being held in different places)
- How to RSVP and the due date
- Your wedding website

JMK TIP

Whatever you've decided is an ideal start time for your ceremony is *not* what you print on the invitations. Just like in theater, guests run late. List a time on the invitation that's 30 minutes before when you intend to actually start the ceremony, a cushion we in the industry refer to as either "invite" (invitee time) or "guest arrival."

Other items often included, but not 100 percent necessary, are these:

- A "reception to follow" note; technically the invitations are to the wedding ceremony, so these words clarify what will happen after (though this is often implied or just not needed)
- The attire (this used to be considered a must on invitations, but it's perfectly acceptable to list this only on your website if words such as "black tie" don't fit well on your invitation design)
- An actual RSVP card with its own envelope (if you're doing everything the printed route)
- A separate card with other details such as directions, parking, or shuttle information
- Your return address on the back of the envelope

The only thing that should not be included on the invitations is your registry. As Miss Mona would say, "It's downright tacky." By including a link to your wedding website, your guests can learn about hotel room blocks and travel recommendations as well as find your registry.

There are all sorts of incredible ways to visually design your invitations and all their components. At Jason Mitchell Kahn & Co., we've mailed items that were nothing short of a work of art! We've sent invitations with wax seals, belly bands, folded designs that must be untied to open, booklets with watercolor drawings of our couples at every venue an event would take place, and gift boxes that had several objects in them. The sky's the limit to what you can do creatively.

I mentioned earlier that the way invitations are made has evolved greatly. It used to be commonly understood that an invitation was only to the ceremony and all other information, such as reception cards, detail cards, and direction cards, belonged elsewhere. Many invitations also included information about other events if everyone

ADVERTISING YOUR SHOW

was invited. Sending an RSVP card with its envelope was a must, and sometimes that allowed people to make their meal selection if required in advance. There's still something fun about opening one of those invitations and looking through all its components, but for various reasons, many couples have simplified this process and send just a single invitation, knowing everything else will be communicated online. I mean, if you have an out-of-towner driving to your event, do you really think they'll use the direction card you send, or will they just plug the address into their map app? Those little RSVP cards can also easily get lost in the mail, and asking your guests to RSVP online draws them to your website for other info.

Listen, I've worked with many people who loved this part of the design process more than anything else. If that's you, then go for it. But in case you're weighing the pros and cons and what can fit into your budget, remember this: The less you have designed and printed, the less you pay.

> **JMK TIP**
>
> Have a design element you love that doesn't quite fit on the invitation? Incorporate it into the envelope liner. That's the first thing a guest sees after they open the flap!

One thing that's absolutely free and what I consider to be vital not to overlook is how you word the invitations. Remember: Back in the day, these came from the bride's parents who invited guests to watch their daughters be given away. Words matter, and most of my clients have felt that traditional invitation language isn't fitting. This is never one-size-fits-all, particularly because you have to consider many factors, including whether it's just the two of you throwing the wedding or it's also with one or both sets of parents. And if either set is divorced but both are contributing, that's another layer to navigate.

Here are some examples of various invitations, with some of my favorite characters filling in for our JMK couples and some supporting reasons the words for each one might work.

1. This is for a couple who's throwing their own wedding as two equals and wants to keep the text simple and drive people to their site to RSVP and for all other info:

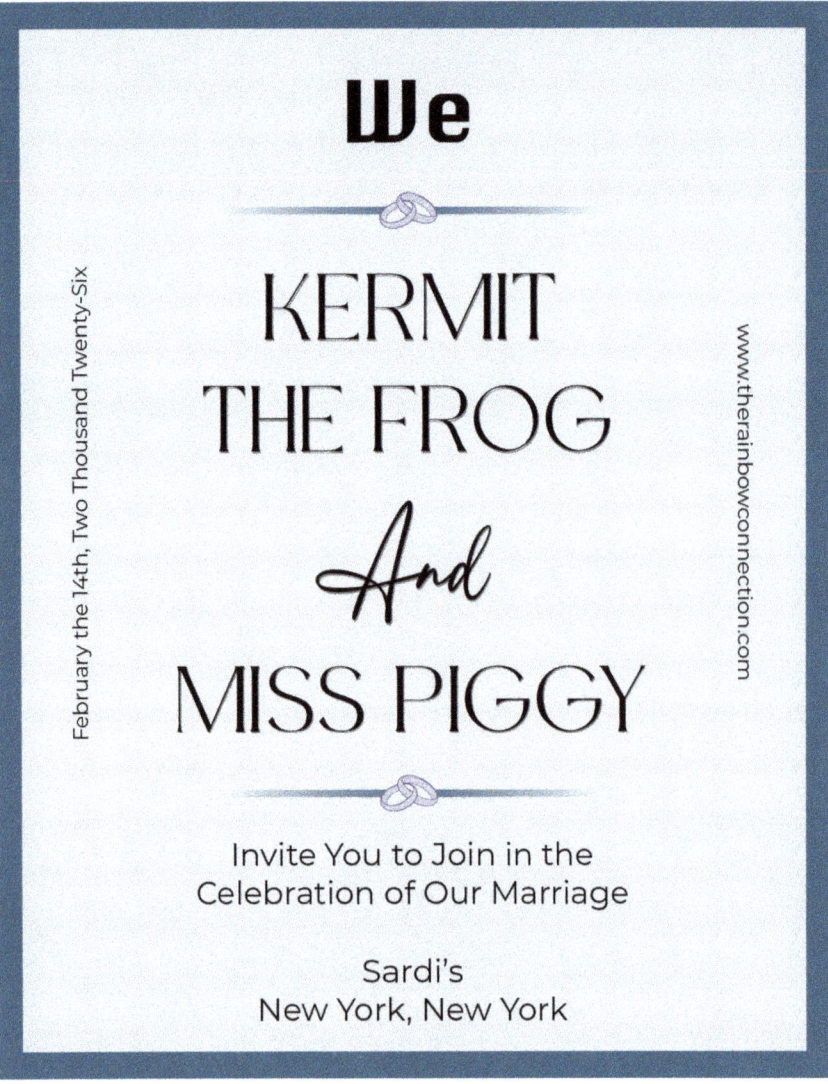

2. This works for a couple that's throwing the wedding with their parents and prefers more verbose text:

WE
ERNIE
— AND —
BERT

TOGETHER WITH OUR FAMILIES
OSCAR COOKIE AND GROVER ELMO
ENTHUSIASTICALLY INVITE YOU
TO BE A PART OF OUR
WEDDING CELEBRATION

SATURDAY THE TWENTIETH
OF JULY AT 5.30 IN THE EVENING

THE STOOP
123 SESAME STREET
NEW YORK, NY 10023

3. This works for a couple whose parents are throwing the wedding and prefer a more formal tone:

Miss Sophia Petrillo

and

Mr. Big Daddy Hollingsworth

Request the Honor of Your Presence
at the Marriage of Their Daughters

Dorothy Zbornak

&

Blanche Devereaux

ON SUNDAY THE TWENTY-FIFTH OF MAY AT
6151 RICHMOND STREET
MIAMI BEACH, FL

RECEPTION TO FOLLOW
AT THE RUSTY ANCHOR

4. This works for a couple who really want to convey a sense of humor:

5. This works for a couple who's marrying on a holiday and is also very into theater:

Hey you! Put the candelabra down for like one second and come to our wedding!

Who:

Christine Daae
(the pretty one)

&

Raoul Vicomte de Chagny
(the rich one, but also pretty)

When:
Saturday, December 31st at midnight

Where:
The lobby stairs of the Paris Opera House

Wear your best masque and come celebrate our union and the new year and watch out for falling chandeliers! (JK. But no, really.)

SUPPORTING ELEMENTS

While the invitations are what matter most, don't forget to consider the supporting elements, whether they're being printed or done digitally.

■ RSVP Cards

Whether you opt for printed RSVP cards or a section on your site, the information should tell the guests their deadline for responding; four weeks before the event is standard, but this can be adjusted as needed. Also if needed, include a place for guests to write their names, tell you whether they're coming, and make their menu selection (if you need to know in advance for catering purposes). Don't forget to look back at your contract with your venue or caterer to see what your due date is for submitting numbers, and be sure to build yourself a cushion. You can also request simple information, such as dietary restrictions, or make it a bit fun, such as a must-have song to play.

- Something traditional would be this:

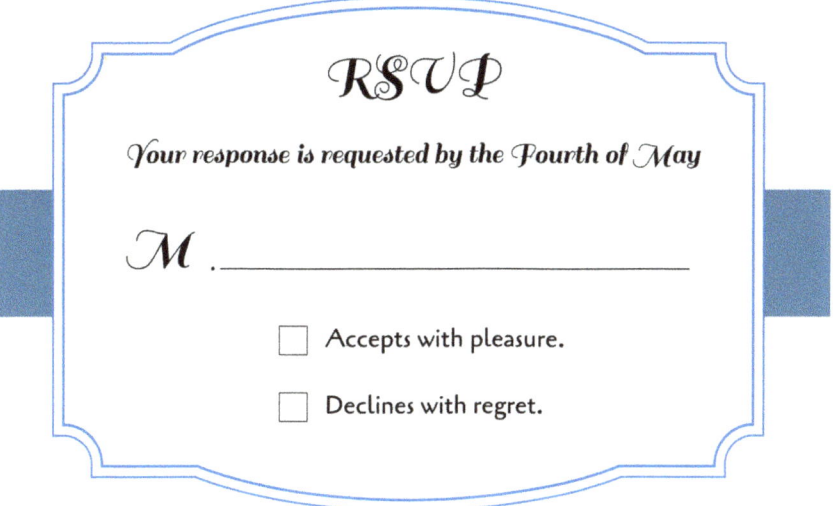

- Something less formal would be this:

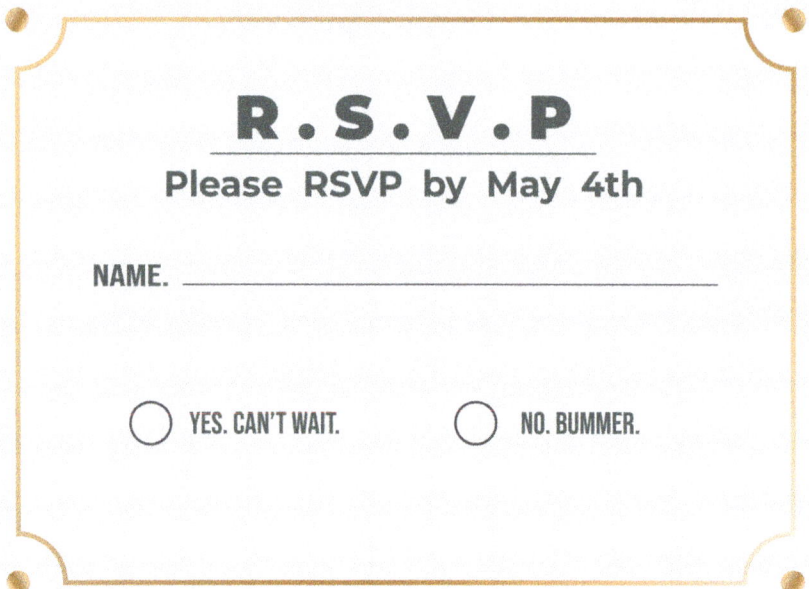

- Something less traditional would be this:

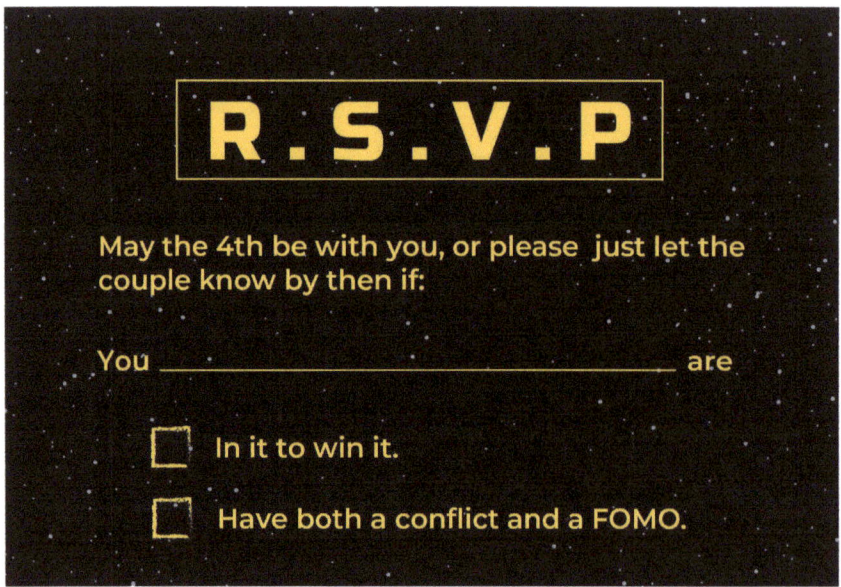

- Something campy that also asks for a meal choice would be this:

R.S.V.P

Hello everybody, my name is ....
What's your RSVP?

☐ I'm coming out. I want the world to know.

☐ And I am telling you I'm not going.

☐ Moo ☐ Cluck ☐ The sound of vegetables growing.

Please return the campiest reply card ever by May 4th

- Something from a couple who wants to incorporate their pet would be this:

R.S.V.P

It doesn't matter whether you love them,
Just put your paws up
Because my parents are getting married!

🐾 _____

☐ Ooh, there ain't no other way!

☐ I'll hide myself in regret.

Barnaby Mitchell Kahn requests your woof by May 4!

If you're sending printed RSVP cards, you'll need to include a stamped envelope in which they'll be returned. These should be pre-addressed to whomever will be doing the tallying, whether it's the two of you, one of your parents, or a bestie. If you look back at the Guest List tab in the workbook, you'll see there are columns to keep track of RSVPs, meals (if needed), and gifts as they begin to arrive.

■ Direction Cards

Think of direction cards as more of a parking or transportation card or section on your site if you're organizing anything that needs explaining, such as whether you're providing shuttle service. You can also recommend taking ride shares and let people know where they're easily available.

■ Reception Cards

If your reception and ceremony are in different locations, you'll need a reception card that lists the where, when, and how of the reception.

■ Envelopes

Once you've selected your invitations and what accompanies them, you'll need to put the names and addresses of your guests on the envelopes. The oldest tradition is formal calligraphy, but that's often the most expensive option because you have to pay someone to address each envelope by hand. Much less expensive printing options can have a similar effect, such as having your chosen font engraved, embossed, raised, or simply printed on the envelopes. Always order extra blank envelopes to give yourself a cushion for mistakes. The envelopes also receive wear and tear from being handled by the postal service, so keep that in mind if you fall in love with an expensive envelope.

JMK TIP

Can't bear the thought of guests receiving a damaged envelope? Put the guest names on the nice envelope that's part of your suite and then pack the entire thing in a postal envelope or box to preserve the quality of its contents. You can even add tracking to double-check that each one has been received.

■ **POSTAGE**

Once you have a sample of your complete invitation, weigh it and find out what the appropriate postage is, which can vary not only by its weight but also by its shape. Then, browse through stamp options and try to find something that feels like the same style. If you're sending digital invitations, see whether there's a way you could customize this element to your aesthetics.

JMK TIP

You can physically go into a post office to see what stamps are currently being sold, but the internet is lined with vendors selling more unique options that might work better with your style.

OTHER PRINTED MATERIALS

Though you might want to arrange for other printed materials, you don't need to do this while you're designing your invitations. But since we're on the subject . . .

■ PROGRAMS

Programs inform guests on how the ceremony will run. They're one of the first things your guests will see at the event, so they should set the tone for what's to come. Like everything else in wedding planning, there are no rules here, but programs should include any or all of the following elements:

- A cover listing *the wedding* of the couple with the *date and location*
- A list of the *wedding party* and the music they're walking to for the processional and recessional
- A list of *what to expect* in the ceremony, such as readings, songs, and the exchange of vows
- An explanation of any *traditions* (old or new) you're incorporating that aren't explained during the ceremony
- A *remembrance section* listing anyone important to either of you who's there only in spirit
- A *welcome note* from the two of you
- A request from the two of you for an *unplugged ceremony*, asking guests to put their phones away
- A *quote* that's meaningful to the two of you
- A *thank-you* page to anyone who has been significant in making your big day happen
- Some *information about your venue* that might be interesting to your guests

Depending on how much information you'd like to offer your guests, there are several options for the layout of your program. It's nice if it mirrors the style of your wedding invitation, but it's not imperative. It can be something practical, such as a program that doubles as a fan for an outdoor ceremony, or you could print a version on a large sign and display it in the pre-ceremony area rather than handing them out individually. If you feel there might be some time to kill, you can make something interactive and fun. I once had a bride request little pencils and inserts next to the programs with her silhouette, along with the following instructions: "Guess the dress. Sketch what you think she might be wearing!"

JMK TIP

Print one program for every two guests. People share, and this will cut your printing costs in half.

■ **ESCORT & PLACE CARDS**

If you have any kind of assigned seating for your meal, which is of course up to you, escort and place cards are necessary. Each escort card lists your guest's name and the table they'll be sitting at. The most expected version of these are tent-style cards folded and displayed neatly on a table. They get the job done, but I'm always searching for ways to be unique with this. The names and table numbers can be printed on a tag and attached to something that doubles as a favor for the guests, something edible or even practical. For a cocktail hour in the Hamptons, we had a raw bar spread and gave every guest their own lobster claw cracker with their name attached. We've also done luggage tags for travelers, seed packets for gardening types, vintage keys for old-timey couples, and printed disks with the guests' names as garnishes for cocktails. If you don't want to produce anything as one per guest or one per couple, you can design a larger format sign or chart. For a very Broadway-inspired wedding we planned, the ceremony program was like a playbill, with all the seating assignments listed as cast lists.

If you want to assign where everyone specifically sits at a table, then you need to have place cards waiting for each guest at their seat. Again, a card will get the job done, but a name on an envelope with a handwritten note from the couple really shows you care! If you're seating people outdoors, be sure the design of this won't blow away.

■ TABLE NUMBERS OR TABLE NAME CARDS

Table numbers or table name cards are how people know which table is which. They can mirror other elements in design, such as having the font for "Table 1" match that of the escort cards, or they can be their own thing. I once planned a wedding for a couple who met in West Hollywood, so we decided to name all the tables after various gay bars in town. We even printed the establishments' logos and framed them. More to come on this when we discuss décor in chapters 9 and 10.

■ MENUS

Menus are a nice touch not only for informing your guests of their meal but for completing the design of your table. Sitting down to a beautiful menu can already make the meal feel more elevated, and at weddings it's difficult to count on the fact that your guests will listen to or be able to hear what the serving staff might be instructed to say. If you're interested in doing place cards, you could double up here and print individual guest names at the top of the menus.

As with everything else, the menus should match your style. They usually wait for guests inside the napkins or on top of the plates or chargers, the decorative larger plate underneath. The top of the menu should say your names and the date, and it's a nice touch to also include a cute quote. If your guests will be choosing their food on the night of, be sure to list all choices on the menu clearly. You can list courses as first, second, and third; appetizer, main, and dessert; to begin, followed by, to finish, and later; Act 1,

Intermission, Act 2, Curtain Call; or any other creative headings you prefer. The menu can also describe the service, such as "all food will be served family style." If the wine you're serving is worth mentioning, then do so. If you'll be moving your guests for one of the courses, you should let them know with something like, "Keep on dancing 'til the world ends. Join us upstairs afterward!"

Even if you're having a cocktail-style meal, you should have a menu that guests can view. This can be on the back of the ceremony program or displayed somewhere they can see it. This will allow guests to know what their options are and pace themselves accordingly. Example language is, "Tonight's dinner will be served cocktail style. That means no assigned seats, but please enjoy our favorite foods from these stations." Cocktail menus are also a nice touch for any bar, especially if you've taken the time to identify some specialty drinks and rename them something cute.

■ NAPKINS & TOWELS

Napkins and towels are details that can definitely make an impression on your guests. A guest towel or napkin that evokes a chuckle in the bathroom while guests are freshening up is always a winner. You can use a logo or other asset you might have designed during the invitation process. I've seen the silhouette of a couple's pet, and we've created some with fun facts, the couples' catch phrases, or just funny quotes. Besides the personalization opportunity, you should see what your venue or caterer provides in the way of napkins and guest towels. If what's provided is suitable to your style, that's fine, but there's nothing worse than using the bathroom at a swanky venue and then drying your hands with something right out of a janitor's closet. If you feel like none of this is speaking to you, then you can always purchase plain ones in your colors.

■ Favor Notes

If you send guests home with a party favor, it's nice to include a note. Since I recommend selecting favors that mean something to you, this note can communicate a last bit of storytelling to your guests, such as "Please enjoy a special treat from where we had our first date" or "Enjoy recovering like we do with our favorite hair of the dog."

■ Other Signage

Anything that requires explanation or a call to action should have a sign explaining it. However, don't create any unnecessary signs just for the sake of it. I've been to weddings where they put out something like a platter of brownies with a sign that just said "brownies." This isn't useful unless you need to differentiate which type of brownies are classic, which contain nuts, and which will take guests on a journey.

There are now several services that allow you to set up an account for guests to upload their photos and videos from the day or night. If this speaks to you, you'll want several signs with QR codes asking your guests to do this. And if there's anything you'd like in a guest book besides a signature, you'll need a sign requesting this, such as "Leave your favorite memory of the couple here or a wish for them to open on their first anniversary." I'm also a fan of signs that aren't directional or instructional but simply personal. Your guests might enjoy washing their hands in the bathroom even more if next to the sink there's a sign that reads, "Shantay, You Stay."

For all these elements, if you really want to forgo printing, you can still have them graphically designed and accessible as a QR code sign your guests can scan and then see all of this on their phones.

■ THANK-YOU CARDS

The final items to consider from your list of printed materials are thank-you cards. It's nice when these match the style of the save the dates or invitations because it bookends the experience for your guests, and you can usually save money when ordering them together. It's also not imperative, and this can be a good opportunity to utilize some of your wedding photos. Etiquette says that guests have up to one year to send a gift, and so do you when it comes to sending thank-you notes. However, I recommend doing it sooner so the gratitude you're feeling is still fresh. The notes you write don't have to be long, but they should be handwritten, from the heart, and signed by both of you.

To help you organize all your advertising components, our workbook includes a Stationery Worksheet you can use to map out all the text. It also accounts for how many different pieces of stationery you need to design and the quantity you'll need for each. Here's an example:

WE DO

STATIONARY TEXT

SAVE THE DATES

QTY: 125
TEXT:

> Save the Date
> Tracy and Link
> July 17, 1962
> Baltimore, MD

INVITATIONS

QTY: 125
TEXT:

> Edna and Wilbur Turnblad
> Invite you to join as their daughter
> Tracy Turnblad
> Ponies her way into a marriage with
> Link Larkin
>
> July 17, 1962
> 5:00 PM
> The Baltimore Ballroom
> Dinner and Dancing to Follow

ADVERTISING YOUR SHOW

CEREMONY PROGRAM

QTY: 75
TEXT:

FRONT:

July 17, 1962
Tracy Turnblad & Link Larkin

PROCESSIONAL
"I Can't Stop Loving You"
Ray Charles

OPENING REMARKS
Motormouth

MOMENT OF SILENCE

EXCHANGING OF VOWS & RINGS

RECESSIONAL
"The Loco Motion"
Little Eva

BACK:

We would like to thank the wedding party for their support and love throughout our lives.

MAID OF HONOR
Penny Lou Pingleton

BEST MAN
Seaweed Stubs

OFFICIANT
"Motormouth" Maybelle Stubbs

STATIONARY TEXT

Do you feel like you've developed a successful advertising campaign for your show or at least gotten the wheels turning to eventually have one? If so, it's time to start thinking about preserving all your hard work. Lights, camera, wedding!

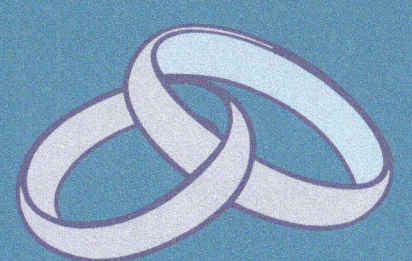

Chapter 6

DOCUMENTING YOUR WORK

You've decided to have an event to celebrate your love, you've worked hard on all the details to plan everything, and then the big day finally arrives. It's one night only! Couples often worry that the feelings of their wedding night will be gone in the morning, and in *Dreamgirls*, Effie White sings about that very feeling. So I do encourage you to be present and in the moment, but if you want the memories to live beyond one night, you must document your show.

PHOTOGRAPHY

With most JMK clients, we try to lock down photographers (and entertainment) right after we book the venue because these vendors can book up quickly and they're an integral part of your show. I cannot emphasize enough the value of quality photography, and it's one of the few elements of your wedding that you get to take with you. If it's within your means, this is not a place to skimp. Professional photography can run the gamut of price ranges.

Photography is an art, and that means it's subjective. Some photographers shoot a grittier candid style, while others compose artistic masterpieces. When viewing a professional's samples, be sure to ask for complete wedding galleries. They may have gotten one incredible shot they posted on Instagram, but it's important you see how they captured the day from start to finish.

There are three equally important steps to identifying the photographer you want to work with:

1. You like their work.
2. Their fee fits your budget.
3. You like their energy, vibe, and personality.

Do not underestimate that third requirement. On your wedding day, your photographer will be around during very intimate and intense moments, so make sure you set yourself up for success.

Now back to the first two.

There are tons of photographers out there, so searching for the right one can be a little exhausting. If you live in a city like I do and ever try to look through the portfolios of every single person who comes up when you Google "wedding photographers," you might immediately throw in the towel on the whole process, so being able to filter your search is helpful. To identify who and what you want, try to get a sense of what type of wedding photography you gravitate toward by asking yourself these questions:

- How would you like your special day documented?
- What kind of pictures do you want to look back at?
- Do you prefer photojournalism and documentary style or traditional and classic?
- Do you want candids, portraits, or a combination?
- Are you okay with digital photography, or are you a stickler for film?
- Would you like your photos in color, black-and-white, or both?

DOCUMENTING YOUR WORK

Photography that resonates with you usually causes some type of emotional response. That's a good thing. When that happens, explore more of their work. It's also important you see someone like the two of you in their work. If you don't, then ask. Not every photographer can have all their work readily available online. And if you're an LGBTQ+ couple or a couple of color and don't see couples like you up front, ask whether they've worked with couples like you before.

If you're feeling overwhelmed by what you're finding online, streamline your search a bit. There's a good chance your venue has a list of photographers who've worked there before that they recommend. Have any of your friends married recently and shown you photos you like? Ask for their recommendations and get the real scoop on what their day was like with them.

Once you've ideally narrowed this down to a small handful of artists, the next step is to see whether you can afford them. Most photographers have a few different packages based on what the takeaways are and how many hours they'll be shooting. If you're unsure which is right for you, talk this through with your photographer and make sure you're aligned on timing. If you dream of having a *Vanity Fair*-inspired shoot with your wedding party, find out how much time your photographer will need to pull that off. Also think about whether you want the photographer at the wedding only, present while you're getting ready, at any of the supporting events, and for an engagement photo shoot.

When you're ready to make this official, ask for a contract. Be sure you read it thoroughly, understand the terms, and confirm the following:

- How many hours do you have them on the wedding day? Be sure it aligns with your expectations. How many people are on their team? Some weddings are fine with just one photographer, while others require a second shooter or more.
- Can you post the images online? We live in a time when being able to share photos of your wedding on social media

might be more important to you than what you might frame in your home. Some photographers won't allow you to post their images unless they're watermarked with their name or logo. It's crucial you understand the terms here. If something isn't right for you, ask the photographer to amend it. If they can't or won't, they might not be the best fit. I understand an artist wanting credit for their work, but there are ways to do that without putting something over an image.

- Will you have the rights to all images or just the ones you purchase?
- Can your guests view and purchase your pictures? Most photographers create an album available for online viewing, and anyone can purchase the prints they'd like to own. If the contract includes this, confirm how long the site will be online, and make sure you're comfortable with the length of time.
- What types of editing do they do in post, if any? We do live in a time when apps and programs can remove blemishes, but your photographer may or may not offer this type of editing.

It's also important to create a timeline for photos that works for everyone. There's an inherent amount of stress before a wedding, and if pictures are running behind schedule, the stress just amplifies. Right before the wedding, your photographer will want what's known as a "shot list," which is a detailed list of the various groupings you'll want for posed photos. I recommend taking all posed photos before the ceremony. Sometimes it's unavoidable, but trying to get in additional family or friend groupings after the ceremony takes away from your time to really enjoy the event. Included in our workbook is a shot list you and your photographer can use as a checklist for any groupings of posed photos you want to ensure are taken, and here's an example:

DOCUMENTING YOUR WORK

	PERSON 1'S SIDE		PERSON 2'S SIDE		COMBINED
☐	Parents	☐	Parents	☐	All Parents
☐	Add Person 2	☐	Add Person 1	☐	All Siblings
☐	Siblings	☐	Siblings	☐	All Grandparents
☐	Add Person 2	☐	Add Person 1	☐	All Cousins
☐	Immediate Family	☐	Immediate Family	☐	Flower Child
☐	Add Person 2	☐	Add Person 1	☐	Ring Bearer
☐	Grandparents	☐	Grandparents	☐	Dog
☐	Add Person 2	☐	Add Person 1	☐	All Wedding Party
☐	Extended Family	☐	Extended Family	☐	
☐	Wedding Party	☐	Wedding Party	☐	
☐	Add Person 2	☐	Add Person 1	☐	

SHOT LIST

When designing your day, think about places that are either meaningful to you or will simply make for cool portraits. It's nice to have variety in your wedding gallery, so doing some pre-ceremony photos elsewhere is ideal. Talented photographers have an eye for these places, but be sure to express your opinion too. I also recommend just the two of you spend some time with the photographer before you start taking the group pictures for the day because it will give you a chance to relax and get comfortable in front of the camera—it's going to follow you around for several hours.

The final photography element I recommend is having an engagement photo shoot. Even if you can't possibly imagine using the images for anything, this is an opportunity to have a trial run with your photographer. It can be a short session in your home or the photographer's studio, or it can be more elaborate, taking place in different locations at different times. Regardless of how extensive the engagement shoot is, it allows you to begin your relationship with the photographer and grow comfortable being in front of them. An engagement shoot also serves as a test run for how you'll look on camera; you might learn you don't like certain angles or facial expressions. And if you get some really fantastic images from the shoot, you can use them for some of your printed materials, such as the save the dates.

VIDEOGRAPHY

For a big chunk of my career, I felt like I was often trying to convince clients to spring for a wedding video. Some couples came in wanting everything including a video, but many felt it was an easy thing to scrap for budgetary or other reasons. I've also seen some videos that were so cheesy they could be labeled as cringeworthy. However, there has been a shift in recent years due to the popularity of sharing short videos on social media, and, yes, that can be an added bonus or a part of what your videographer creates. But first, let's talk more broadly about videography so you can decide whether it's something you want.

DOCUMENTING YOUR WORK

Nothing can replace photography. Videography is meant to be an addition, not an instead of. If you're still on the fence about a video, I encourage you to look to the future. Even if you can't picture yourself ever watching it, one day you might have children who are curious or relatives who couldn't make it and want to see what they missed. Video has the ability to capture tender moments fully, such as your vows, a meaningful toast, and the way your mom danced with your fabulous friends. It also might provide footage you find special when someone who was at your wedding is no longer around.

If you simply cannot swing it with your budget, at least put a dedicated person in charge of getting some footage of your ceremony on their phone. That way you'll still have some sort of record. You can set up a tripod in a location where people won't knock it over but a dedicated phone's camera can still capture the ceremony. If you're booking a professional videographer, it comes with similar guidelines to those for a photographer:

- Ask how many hours they'll be on-site and about the size of their team.
- Identify the type of video you want. Some videographers do a really nice job capturing the night, while others turn them into full documentaries.
- Ask for a sample of their work. Even from watching a stranger's wedding video, you can tell whether you like the way the story was told.
- Ask someone at the wedding venue whether they have recommendations of videographers they've worked with before. Some studios provide both services under one umbrella, but more often they're independent vendors.
- Discuss and confirm the schedule, and make sure it works for everyone involved.
- Be sure you understand the deliverables. Most full wedding videos will be highlights of all the key moments, from getting ready and the ceremony to special dances and toasts. You'll typically have the ability to view the ceremony in full,

and some videographers will also offer you all of the raw footage that doesn't make the edited product.
- Understand the format in which you'll be receiving it. The days of videos being made as DVDs are long gone, so make sure you're comfortable with how you'll be able to view or stream your video.

Once you've booked a videographer, it's important to connect them with your photographer to make sure they're both on the same page. Also, many videographers offer aerial shooting or drone footage, which can make for an excellent result. Just be sure it's allowed at your venue.

One of the reasons this vendor has regained popularity is that most videographers now create short videos that are ideal for sharing on social media. While that's the platform they're designed for, it's important to understand from your videographer when this will be completed. Many couples want content to post right away, and that's usually not something a videographer can do unless agreed to in advance.

CONTENT CREATION

As someone who shares a lot of my work on social media, I totally understand the desire to have content well-suited for it. However, many photographers and videographers I work with have expressed frustration with clients wanting this right away. This has led to a new role of content creation that can sometimes be added on through a photographer or videographer or hired as an independent contractor. Content creators record your wedding, usually right on a phone, and then immediately turn around what they have. If this is important to you, I highly recommend hiring someone to be dedicated to this. I once had a bride spend over thirty minutes in her getting-ready suite being frustrated with the photographer because she wanted to create something based on a current TikTok trend that the photographer was unfamiliar with. If something like this is what you're after, a content creator will be much more adept at guiding you on how to execute it.

FROM STAGE TO SCREEN

Once you have your photos, videos, content, and any other technological documentation, it's time to digitize them. Technology is an ever-changing landscape, but the importance of documenting a fabulous wedding is tried and true. However, this is the topic I was most nervous about writing, mainly because it makes me feel like a dinosaur in a futuristic environment. It's difficult to move ahead and not feel that by the time this goes to print, what I've laid out for you might be completely outdated. While I love my iPhone and use it regularly for work and pleasure, I'm old enough to remember a time when we had devices such as answering machines and Walkmans, which at the time felt cutting-edge. I also remember going on dates with people I met on Friendster and MySpace, but those platforms didn't stand the test of time. Still, we all know technology isn't going anywhere. So, let's focus on how best to utilize it for your wedding and discuss some of the decisions you might want to make around it. This is an area where I'll do my best to stay relevant, heeding the current guidelines on what can be shared online and through various platforms, including my own. So as Rachel Maddow, one of my heroes, often says, "Watch this space."

■ WEDDING WEBSITES & APPS

Having a wedding website has become as common as a new season of *Drag Race*. They're a fantastic place to house all the information relevant to your guests, and best of all, unlike printed invitations, you can update them regularly. Now, if you're technologically challenged, do not fear! Many of the bigger wedding platforms, such as Zola, The Knot, and Minted, offer various website templates for free or a minimal charge. Once you select the style you like, it's a relatively turnkey process.

Most sites also offer the ability to put password protection on your site, so if you want your guests to be able to only view your wedding information, be sure to enable that feature and include the password where you advertise your wedding. You can also code various events for the weekend; some guests might be invited only to the wedding, while others are also invited to the welcome party and/or brunch. If you set up coding, guests will see only what they're invited to. If you enjoy website design or have someone in your circle who does, you can of course start from scratch and make your own.

Wedding websites can be minimal and list just essential information, or they can have more bells and whistles of your personality. Here's what's often included:

- **Home Page**

The home or welcome page of your wedding website can include a note from the two of you, a photo, and even a countdown.

- **Schedule**

The schedule of events should list the time and place for every event taking place. You can list the suggested attire for each event along with relevant travel information, such as a shuttle schedule or parking options.

- **RSVP**

If you're collecting RSVPs on your site, be sure your RSVP page is set up to collect not only the yeses and noes, but anything else you might need, such as meal choices and dietary restrictions.

- **Accommodations**

The accommodations section or page of your website should include all important information about what you've arranged for your guests, such as hotel room blocks with the direct links to your blocks and when their cutoff dates are. You can also include suggestions for other housing options.

- **Registry**

Include on your registry page the links to what you've organized for your registry, including physical gifts, funds people can contribute to, and organizations or causes you're raising money for.

- **FAQs**

Your FAQs page serves to answer in more detail what's on people's minds, such as your policy about children. It's also an ideal space to let your guests know anything that might influence what they wear or bring for it, such as the ceremony being outside.

There are other pages you might want to include but are less of a necessity and more about the fun of it all:

- **The Story of the Two of You**

Your "The Story of Us" page can begin with how you met, the life you've already been building together, and the details of your engagement.

- **The Wedding Party**

Include a place on your site where you can share photos, bios, and explanations of how each person in your wedding party is connected.

- **Things to Do**

Suggest what guests who are traveling in for your wedding might want to spend their non-wedding time doing.

Some wedding website platforms are also available as apps, and there are apps that serve other purposes beyond what we just discussed, such as group messaging platforms. If you're planning to use one, it's best to utilize a platform that can get information out via texting without your guests needing to download the app. If there's a road closure that might affect traffic or a place where a shuttle will pick up guests, a group messaging platform dedicated to this is ideal. If it's a platform where guests can ask questions and might need fast replies, put someone else in charge of managing this. You'll have enough to think about already, and this can help relieve some pressure.

■ SOCIAL MEDIA

In no way can I write as an expert on how to use social media, but since it's a part of every industry, I urge you to think about it and how you want to use it at your wedding, if at all.

As an example of how quickly social media changes, let's discuss hashtags. When they first gained popularity, it became a growing trend for engaged couples to come up with unique hashtags for their weddings, and we had a lot of fun getting creative with them. But besides figuring out rhymes with a couple's names or some other pun, hashtags serve a purpose: When a photo is posted with a hashtag, the hashtag takes viewers to all the other photos with the same tag. When Instagram was only a place for grid posts, this was common, but when Instagram Stories came along, whether a photo was posted on them with the hashtag or not, the photo was gone twenty-four hours later. This eventually led to the popularity of QR codes and other photo-collecting prompts, sadly making all the creative hashtags less relevant.

There are a few platforms that allow you to go live, and this is a chance to let those not attending see parts of the wedding as they happen in real time, such as your first dance. And you might want parts of your wedding to go viral

DOCUMENTING YOUR WORK

on social media but not want your wedding shared with all your guests' followers. Think about the scenarios and outcome you want. If it's to have as much reach as possible, you might want to provide instructions for who to tag so you can repost easily. Maybe you're somewhere in the middle and don't mind whether your wedding is shared but would prefer it didn't happen while guests were still at the wedding. In that case, include a sign at the ceremony asking guests not to post until after the wedding. You could also create custom filters and GIFs. You do you!

■ DEVICES

Our cell phones, tablets, smart watches, and other technological devices go hand in hand with producing social media, and they can be the best or worst accessory for your guests depending on how you feel. Most of us are addicted to our devices in some way, and it's challenging to behave any differently, even at well-produced events. If people having their phones out and in use throughout your wedding doesn't bother you, that's fine, but many JMK couples have expressed frustration with this topic. When you walk down the aisle, do you want to look out and see your guests' smiling faces, or do you want to see a room full of people trying to film you on their phones? If you'd prefer the former, that's what we refer to as an "unplugged ceremony." Asking guests to be off their phones during the ceremony is quite common, as it forces them to be more present with you and leaves the documentation of the experience to the pros you've hired. Taking this one step further, some couples prefer their wedding to be truly phone free and thus require a phone check. Similar to what's done in some schools and live performance events, guests are asked to seal their phones in a bag that can't be unlocked until guests step outside or leave.

Not too long ago, I attended a seminar about technology as part of a global wedding conference, where I learned about the use of virtual reality glasses in wedding events. Restaurants provide them to guests, who then sit for a multicourse meal while being transported around the world to experience various cuisines. The speaker said we should expect such virtual experiences to become more common at weddings, but it's too soon to tell whether that's true. Currently that would be a massive financial commitment for couples, and even if the cost comes down and the accessibility goes up, I'm not sure virtual reality events are the right fit for JMK couples. However, there's always Zoom.

JMK TIP

If you know some people who can't attend in person but would like to witness your event, arrange to have the ceremony available on Zoom so they can watch it in real time. Just be sure someone other than you is in charge of setting this up and running it!

Technology is certainly a tool that has improved the efficiency of many wedding planning tasks, but there's also something to be said about the real-time experiences JMK couples create for their guests. Weddings will always be about bringing a couple's communities together and sharing in a one-time-only experience, and technology will never be able to replace the feeling in a room during a ceremony, the love shared at a big table over a special meal, or the pulse of a dance floor. I might have just aged myself. Technology can be like a wedding itself: It's best when it brings people together.

DOCUMENTING YOUR WORK

Did you complete your shot list and discuss your preferences on the use of technology at your wedding? Do you feel you have a good understanding of your and your paparazzi's needs here and are ready to dive into the next subject? I'll meet you in the sound booth!

Chapter 7

COMPOSING THE SCORE

Any well-written show needs an accompanying score from beginning to end. Music is a critical element of how you make your event really come alive, so you only want to book something that's aligned with your vision and tastes. A YouTube search of "wedding bands" or "wedding DJ" might have you dreaming of a wedding in complete silence. There's lots of crappy entertainment out there, but there are also tons of incredible artists who can make your show really sing.

Let's go back to the initial vision. Is yours a wedding with a packed dance floor, or is it more of a dinner party with music that supports that vibe? Will there be a chance for guests to lip sync for their lives? I've planned just about every version of this, and like everything else, it's about what's best for you.

While there are more options for music besides a band or a DJ, those are the two most common to choose from. And as you've probably already guessed, there's a huge budgetary difference between the two. Let's unpack everything about them.

BANDS

In case you haven't been paying attention to anything I've been saying, I'm a lover of performing arts. To me, there's nothing like the energy that comes from live music at a wedding, unless the band isn't so good. When searching for a band to play your wedding, start with what's right for the reception and add on from there. Some bands automatically include musicians to cover the ceremony and the cocktail hour, some offer à la carte add-ons, and some need to be booked separately.

Most wedding bands I've hired that will play music for large dance sets usually have eight to twelve people. If you really want something like an expanded horn section, opt to add additional musicians. If you're looking at any type of smaller group, keep in mind that they probably can't cover as much of a range of music as larger bands. If you don't have a good sense of what the right fit is for you, the only way to get started is by listening. Most bands have ample online videos of their work. Some also have regular gigs you can go to, and some participate in showcases geared toward prospective couples. If seeing a band perform live is an option, I highly recommend doing so. I've witnessed several bands whose live energy, vibe, and sound was absolutely incredible but just couldn't be captured similarly on video. Some bands might also invite you to one of their sound checks, or you can ask other couples for referrals and opinions.

If an established wedding band isn't speaking to you, you can contemplate other musical groups that aren't known for doing weddings. It's great to think creatively, but be careful about hiring people who are inexperienced in what you need. Living in New York, I've heard amazing musicians everywhere, from cabaret venues to subway platforms, but that doesn't necessarily mean they could do a wedding. You'll also want a group that's proficient in performing a variety of music.

If you find a band you like, there are some important things to review in the contract:

COMPOSING THE SCORE

- **Know the Breakdown of Musicians and Singers**
  If you fall in love with a certain person in a band, you can ask for them to be assigned to your wedding. Most contracts state they can never guarantee this 100 percent. That's normal, because if the diva you fell in love with loses her voice, trust me, you want the understudy.

- **Confirm the Length of Time They'll Play Live**
  A reception contract with a band is usually for four hours, and the ceremony and the cocktail hour are separate. For the reception, see whether they require breaks in their contract and, if so, how they handle them. All musicians need a break, which is reasonable. Some bands will rotate breaks so that you always have some live music playing, while others prefer to put on a few prerecorded tracks and break the band as a group. And while some bands will do your ceremony and your cocktail hour and rotate different musicians and instruments throughout the night, others will do only the reception. Ask what the cost of overtime will be in case you want to extend.

- **Find Out Their Policy on Learning New Songs**
  Most bands will learn a few new songs that aren't in their repertoire, but if your requests are huge, perhaps the band isn't the right fit.

- **Look Into Vendor Meals**
  Most caterers or venues can provide meals for the vendors, but be sure to plan for this in advance. The band might list this in what's known as a "rider." Are there any other requests that will need to be sourced? Not all caterers have fresh ginger to go in hot water, especially without having it prearranged!

- **Check for Space Requirements**
  Some bands require a green room or certain dimensions for the performance area. Make sure you can accommodate. You don't want to hire a band that shows up and refuses to play because the stage is too small.

- **Confirm Equipment Needs and Power Sources**
  Ask whether any additional sound equipment will be needed and, if so, whether they provide it or you're responsible. Double-check with your venue to make sure the power available is suitable for your band. The only blackouts should be by drunk people!

- **Ask About Lighting**
  The band needs to be lit, and if your venue doesn't have the necessary lighting, maybe the band can work with you here. You don't want to pay to have them in the dark. If they do have their own lighting, find out what it is and make sure you like it. You don't want any surprise disco balls!

- **Make Sure Their Setup Needs Are Feasible**
  Most bands need time for a sound check, but make sure it's reasonable and within your timeline and at your venue. Also make sure they can set up appropriately in each location. Many bands have clauses in their contracts related to taking equipment up steps or laying it on cobblestones, on grass, and in the sun.

- **Ask What Their Options Are for Attire**
  You can go formal with gowns and white dinner jackets, or you can have an entire group in sequined onesies. Better yet, maybe they change looks halfway through the night. Whatever fits your style!

>
> **JMK TIP**
>
> If you're having trouble finding a band well-suited to the entire reception, identify what you want most out of them and hire them for less time. I had a couple obsessed with nineties rock, so we found an incredible small group called "Saved by the 90s." We knew four hours would be overkill, so we hired them just to play after dinner and used a playlist beforehand.

DJs

Regardless of all the conversations I've had with JMK couples about my love of live music, many have told me they prefer their favorite songs sung by the artists who created them. I also spent most of my twenties hanging out at gay bars, so I can appreciate a good DJ too. Whether it's a budgetary or style decision, a DJ might be a better fit for you.

Just as with a band, try to see a DJ in action before you hire them. If the DJ you're interested in hasn't done weddings before, make sure you're able to discuss your vision for the night and get what you want. Some DJs are amazingly accommodating, while others feel it's their way or no way. It's your wedding, not their club booking!

Once you've found a DJ you like, there are some important things to review in their contract:

- **What Are the Equipment Requirements?**
  Do they provide their own equipment, or does the venue have the equipment the DJ will use? You could easily double the cost of the DJ if they have a list of additional equipment they'll need you to rent. Also, will they handle placing the order for equipment or do they expect you to?

- **What Will They Be Wearing?**
  Style is subjective, but make sure theirs suits your vision.

- **Will They Provide Lighting and, If So, What Is It?**
  Make sure they don't have a competing vision from yours!

- **How Long Will You Have Them?**
  Ideally a DJ covers cocktail hour, even if it's just a playlist, and they play your selected music during the ceremony.

- **How Long Will It Take Them to Set Up?**
  Sometimes DJ's show up as one-person operations, and if they're setting up sound equipment in three different locations, it's important they aren't scrambling to complete this on time.

FINDING HARMONY

Regardless of whether you hire live musicians or a DJ, there are some important things to review with them in advance:

- **Give Them a Playlist**
  You should have the music you want at your wedding, so the more specific you are with your playlist, the better. Remember: You're hiring people to work for you. Our workbook includes a Playlist Worksheet where you can list the specific songs you'd like for certain moments.

- **Make Them a "Do Not Play" List!**
  Do certain songs you hear at weddings make you cringe? Are there songs that trigger bad memories for either of you? No need to relive the breakup song that you identify with an ex, so let your musicians know!

COMPOSING THE SCORE

- **Confirm the Timeline**

  A few weeks before, schedule a time to go over the detailed timeline of your event with the musicians. You are designing the flow of the night, and they are hired to execute it. Again, the more detailed you can be, the better. Do you want to kick off the reception with everyone dancing, or is the party music reserved for the last hour? Be very clear on the logistics of the event. What's their timeline for setup? Is there parking available for them? Is there a separate entrance at your venue they need to load in and out from? Confirming details like this is especially vital if your venue is off the beaten path. No need to be stressed on your special day because the musicians are late.

- **Make Sure They're Properly Prepared**

  The bandleader or DJ serves as your emcee for the night, so go over the style you want them to have in the way they interact with your guests. They should speak only when there are special announcements, not act as the host of a reality competition. Give them phonetic spellings for any names that might be difficult to pronounce, and review what announcements you want made. Be very specific with the wording. Many of us are quite particular in the labels we use to describe our status. You don't want the musicians welcoming you to the dance floor using titles you don't identify with!

- **Make Sure They Have a Point of Contact the Night Of**

  Your point of contact for music should not be you! It's crucial during the ceremony and throughout the night to keep the event on the schedule you've designed. You don't want the mother–son dance getting started when both mother and son are using the bathroom!

- **Ensure They're Prepared to Play a Variety of Music**
  Yes, the night is all about the two of you, but you also want to cater to all your guests.

- **Don't Micromanage Their Choices**
  Yes, I empower you to give your musicians all sorts of input to make this a reflection of you, but you're also hiring them to read the room and respond organically to the energy of the crowd.

JMK TIP

Love live music but can't afford a band? Pair a live musician, such as a saxophonist, with your DJ. It brings the energy of live music to the room without the price tag of a full group.

OTHER OPTIONS

If all of this is too much for you, don't be afraid. I've attended smaller-scale weddings that were a blast with curated playlists. If this is what you have available, follow all the same guidelines for DJs when selecting the music you want programmed. Create different lists for the various elements of the night, including guest arrival, the ceremony, the cocktail hour, dinner, and dancing. Make sure there's adequate equipment to amplify the sound. Most importantly, put a friend in charge of operating this throughout the night. Even at a small and simple affair, the two of you should not be working the music.

THE ORCHESTRATION

Your wedding day is a story to be told, and it needs the right soundtrack to execute and enhance it. Whether you have ceremony musicians, a band, a DJ, a self-made playlist, or any combination of the above, there are some important guidelines for selecting your music for the different parts of the event.

■ ACT 1: THE CEREMONY

Having live musicians orchestrate a ceremony is extremely common at weddings, and depending on what kind of event you're designing, this might be either right on the money or incredibly far off the mark for you. Strings are the most popular type of instrument, be it a quartet, a trio, or even just an independent harp or cello. It's also common to have someone playing an acoustic guitar or a piano to set a vibe.

If any of this feels too old-timey for you, keep in mind that you don't have to have a string quartet play "Ave Maria." Classical versions of contemporary songs are a fun way to give this tradition a spin. I was once in a wedding party for a couple who booked a hip, gay DJ, and we walked the processional to a song by Goldfrapp and the recessional to "Like a Virgin" by Madonna. The guests laughed and cheered and knew they were headed to a super-fun reception. It was an accurate reflection of the couple.

Whatever you choose for your music source, you can create a beautiful, customized ceremony soundtrack with the songs you select. Whether you're going for sentimentality, humor, irony, romance, or lessons in camp, think of the story you're telling and what you want your guests to feel as you select. Here are components to think about assigning music to:

- **Pre-Ceremony or Prelude**

  Music should be playing at all moments of the event other than when someone is speaking. It begins with what's heard while guests first arrive, which usually starts about thirty minutes before the ceremony. It's the first sound of the event and sets the tone, and this can be a good place to incorporate music the two of you like that simply doesn't fit anywhere else.

- **Processional**

If you or anyone in your wedding party is walking down the aisle, you need at least one song for them and one, if not two, for the two of you. This depends on the order of your cast list from chapter 4. For larger groups, you can have a few songs that change throughout. In traditional weddings, there's always a song change before the bride enters, and it's reserved only for her walk down the aisle. We've also used one song for the entirety of a processional, waiting for the dramatic key change toward the end for the couple to enter together. Typically, a processional is done without any vocals, but we've sometimes incorporated singers because, why not? That being said, this is the overture for Act 1, so it should be in line with the story you want to tell. Funny, dramatic, sentimental, campy or very traditional are all viable options!

- **Ceremony Orchestrations**

Some ceremonies have no music other than the processional and recessional, while some are completely orchestrated or have only certain moments that are. Designing a soundtrack for the entire ceremony can create a beautiful effect, but it's also an enormous undertaking. Remember: The more elaborate you make your ceremony and its sound cues, the more requirements at rehearsal and sound check.

- **Ceremony Performances**

In addition to someone performing spoken word, it's common for there to be a musical performance during the ceremony. Usually this stems from having a vocally talented guest in attendance. If this is fitting for you, make sure you can agree with the performer on the song choice. If your guest is going to perform with your musicians, help them arrange a rehearsal in advance. You'll also need to take care of any necessary equipment, such as an extra mic or a music stand. I've also worked with couples who wanted some type of singalong as part of their ceremony. For something involving the entire crowd, be sure the lyrics are printed in the program so everyone can participate. It was a little cheesy but, honestly, also so sweet to see everyone swaying and singing "The Rainbow Connection."

- **Recessional**

For the recessional, you just need to pick one song that feels right for the moment. The two of you will be glowing from having just said your vows, exchanged rings, and kissed. Any friends or family who walked down the aisle before you will follow you now. What's next? Cocktail hour? What mood do you want to put your guests in? The song choice for the recessional is also a great opportunity for a bit of humor and festivity.

JMK TIP

Regardless of what route you go for ceremony music, be sure to account for all the required ceremony audio. Even if you're having tracks played through a speaker, it's incredibly important your guests can hear the ceremony well. Outdoor ceremonies require greater amplification because they often have competing background noise.

■ INTERMISSION: COCKTAIL HOUR

If you're having a cocktail hour that leads into your reception, it's best to choose music that will differentiate it from both the ceremony and the party that will follow. Cocktail hour is a time for guests to mingle, not dance. A jazz trio is the most common here, but again, they don't have to play expected jazz standards. This isn't the dance section of the night, so if there's another genre of music you like that doesn't quite fit elsewhere, this is a perfect time. On more than one occasion, I've hired a group in New York that solely does bluegrass renditions of showtunes!

■ ACT 2: THE RECEPTION

Time to get this party started! You're officially entering act 2 of your show, and the music played at your reception is the glue between all the beats. No need for all the clichéd music you've heard about at cookie-cutter weddings. (Yes, there are weddings that actually still do the chicken dance, the electric slide, and the macarena!). As you make song choices for the highlighted moments of your reception and for the list you provide for dance sets, ask yourself what your favorite songs are and what will be popular with your guests.

● Kickoff

What's the very first song you want your guests to hear at the reception? If they're entering from another space after cocktail hour, this is the music that beckons them in and sets the tone. Do you want to ease them in or tell them from the start that it's time to party? Think about what moment you're building the energy for. Are you about to have a first dance where you want everyone screaming and cheering, or is a gentler moment approaching? Also consider whether after your entrance you'll be encouraging everyone to join you on the dance floor or sit for their meal first. The feeling you want to convey should influence the tone of what songs play during this time. Keep in mind that your caterer might insist they have an opportunity to take guests' food orders before bringing you in, in which case you don't want guests to feel like they should be dancing.

- **Entrance & First Dance**

We discussed what words might be said if you're introduced, but what about the song that accompanies the announcement? Depending on the song you've picked, it could be played during just the entrance, or it could be played during both the entrance and the first dance. You're not obligated to have this kind of revelry, but this is how the reception gets started. In terms of a first dance, if you're doing one, you don't have to dance to the entirety of a song. You can, but you can also keep it to just a verse and a chorus, then either have the song fade or invite guests to join you on the dance floor.

- **Family Dances**

If you're having a father–daughter, mother–son, or any other fabulous combination of family dance together, it can be such a sweet moment for you and your guests. However, I've had plenty of clients who've told me one of their parents was very shy and wouldn't enjoy being the center of attention. In those cases, they still danced together, it just wasn't preceded by a big announcement to get everyone's attention. For song choices, I recommend something that's personal to you and the members of the family involved. Again, funny, sentimental, significant, or plain campy all work as options. And in this book where we're not super focused on gender, I have to share a beautiful new tradition we've done at a few of my LGBTQ+ weddings: mother–daughter and father–son dances. These are special moments of acceptance and love that move everyone who's in the room.

- **Cake Cutting**

If you're including the cake-cutting ritual, be sure to pick the right song to orchestrate it. I find when people choose songs such as "Sugar, Sugar" or "Cake by the Ocean," it's a bit obvious and uninspired. Remember: Everything is an opportunity to be personal. People will see you're cutting a cake, so you don't need the lyrics to spell this out. The cutting is celebratory, so you can use that as a guideline. Think about the two of you and what you're celebrating!

- **Last Dance**

After all the eating, drinking, dancing, laughing, crying, and celebrating, what final moment do you want your guests to leave with? Something inspirational, humorous, or personal? Do you want the entire crowd to be dancing with you or for everyone to be watching as the two of you share the last moments of your wedding? I truly have no idea why having a drunken crowd doing a kick line to "New York, New York" became popular for this, but yes, it's still something people choose. I've seen "Seasons of Love," "Don't Stop Believin'," and "Love on Top" be popular, crowd-pleasing choices. And of course, Donna Summer's "Last Dance" never goes out of style!

- **Ethnic Traditions**

Depending on your heritage and whether you're choosing to honor any part of it, there are certain traditional dances you might want to include:

COMPOSING THE SCORE

◆ **Hora**

The hora is a circle dance commonly performed at Jewish weddings. It usually combines the songs "Hava Nagila" and "Siman Tov u'Mazel Tov," increasing in tempo throughout. The married couple is lifted in chairs while they each hold one side of a handkerchief or napkin. Sometimes the parents and siblings of the couple are also lifted.

> **JMK TIP**
>
> If you're doing a hora at your wedding, be sure to confirm with the band or DJ how many people are expected to be lifted up in chairs. It should be decided in advance whether anyone besides the two of you will be lifted. It's traditional for the parents to be raised as well, but it shouldn't be forced on anyone who's opposed. With this information, the band or DJ can cue the next moment after the chair section is complete.

◆ **Mezinka or Mezinke**

Also from Jewish culture, the mezinka is meant to honor the parents who just married off their last child. It's a different type of circle dance where the parents are seated in the middle of the dance floor and the married couple presents them with flower crowns. From there, each guest goes up to the parents to say mazel tov. As someone who has attended and planned many Jewish weddings, I've still never seen this in person.

◆ Tarantella

The Tarantella is also a circular dance, this one popular in Italian cultures, and it's intended to bring good fortune to a couple.

◆ Kalamatiano

A folk dance from Greek culture, the kalamatiano also involves guests getting into a circle, in this case with their hands on one another's shoulders. It's often the first dance at a Greek wedding.

◆ Hasapiko

Though popular in both Turkish and Greek cultures, the hasapiko emanates from the latter. It can be seen in the opening sequence of *My Big Fat Greek Wedding*, and it translates to "the butcher's dance," though now it's done without the weapons.

● Specialty Acts

Do you want to add a little more to your party musically to create some unforgettable moments that will truly wow your guests? New Orleans-inspired second-line bands can be a fabulous way to engage the whole crowd. They're ideal if you're literally marching your guests from one place to the next, be it from a ceremony to a cocktail hour or a reception to an after-party. I've also hired Samba bands for a couple who wanted a nod to their Brazilian heritage but not have that be the only type of music for the night.

If you have a talented guest attending who wants to sing but the ceremony isn't quite right for that, they can have a moment in the spotlight during the reception. It could have a dual purpose, such as singing during your

COMPOSING THE SCORE

first dance, or it can be its own entertainment, such as a rousing number to conclude dinner and transition to dancing.

OTHER ENTERTAINMENT

I've had a lot of fun in my career with couples who've wanted to further decorate their weddings with various performances. It's wonderful to be greeted with champagne as you enter a reception, and it's even more fabulous if it's being poured for you by an aerialist from above. Are you interested in surprising your guests? Statues that appear nonhuman and suddenly emerge near an escort display, as well as a wall with gloved hands coming out of it that were holding beverages, have also been big hits. For a very New York-inspired wedding, we had dancing taxicabs that appeared after the cake cutting. We've also had go-go boys, mermaids in bathtubs, and contortionists with disco balls for heads. If these types of acts interest you, I highly recommend going for one. Guests absolutely love this unexpected touch to a wedding.

As someone who has planned many queer weddings, I've hired many drag queens, which probably comes as no surprise to you. The art of drag is absolutely beloved in our community, so why would we *not* want it to be part of our weddings? For the right audience, a medley by a drag queen can really take an event to the next level, especially when it's timed at a moment when you want to raise the energy level. If you go this route, it's very important that the entrance be well-thought-out to make the most of the moment. I've staged them to catch a bouquet, pop out of a cake, and even arrive dressed as brides at the wrong wedding. For a theatrical set of grooms in New York City, we had a local queen do "Music and the Mirror" from *A Chorus Line* in the Cassie dress, and the crowd went wild. It's all about knowing your audience!

JMK TIP

If you want to create the vibe of a drag show at a gay bar where guests are tipping the queen, be sure to take out singles in advance and provide them for your guests. Most people barely carry cash anyway, let alone to a wedding.

Now that you've learned about the many options and guidelines for your show's musical score, it's again time to visit the workbook and fill in the Music Map document. Here's a sample of a musical breakdown:

COMPOSING THE SCORE

MUSIC CUES	PLAYLIST REQUESTS	DO NOT PLAYS
Ceremony	**Pre Ceremony**	**Pre Ceremony**
Wedding Party Processional Thank You For Being a Friend	Anything Bridgerton Style Ella Fitzgerald Blossom Dearie	Pomp & Circumstance Fiddler on the Rood Phantom of the Opera
Wedding Party Second Song Who Runs the World	**Cocktail Hour**	**Cocktail Hour**
Final Entrance Processional Simply the Best	Postmodern Jukebox Pink Martini	Frank Sinatra
Recessional I Drove All Night		
Reception	**Dinner**	**Dinner**
Wedding Party Entrances For the Gaze	Shirley Bassey Select Showtunes Adele Dolly Parton	Carrie Underwood
Couple's Entrance Murder on the Dance Floor	**Dance Floor Musts**	**Dance Floor Must Nots**
First Dance All the Lovers	Whitney Gaga Madonna Dua Lipa Ariana Celine Cher Let's Have a Kiki Mr. Brightside Gloria	Black Eyed Peas Anything The Twist I've Had the Time of my Life Don't Stop Believin
Family Dance Mother My Best Girl		
Family Dance Father My Heart Belongs to Daddy		
Cultural The Hora		
Traditions Single Ladies		
Cake Cutting Espresso		
Last Dance Love on Top		

MUSIC MAP

WE DO

We've discussed a lot about music and entertainment, so do you feel inspired to dance on over to many a couple's favorite part of planning? I'll see you for the oysters and open bar!

Chapter 8

THE CONCESSIONS

In the words of Oscar Wilde, "After a good dinner one can forgive anybody, even one's own relatives."[1] But in planning a wedding, we're not seeking to create a good meal for the sake of forgetting all the rest; we're selecting a menu that enhances your event and continues to tell your story. The negative connotations associated with "wedding food" are unnecessary. Regardless of your budget, you can plan a fabulous menu that makes an impression on your guests. It's all in the details.

FOOD

As you work to select your menu, look for items that strike a balance between being creative and being crowd-pleasing enough to suit all your guests. But before you can get into drizzles and dusts, you must decide what kind of menu you'll serve. This will mainly be determined by your budget, but it's also determined by the time of day and your preference for how the event will flow. Here are the ABCs of your options:

■ APPETIZERS & HORS D'OEUVRES

If you're having a cocktail hour, you'll need to serve some food to accompany the drinks, such as passed appetizers (also known as canapés) and/or stations. Cocktail hour is a wonderful opportunity to incorporate your favorite foods. Even if you're having a fancy affair, mini grilled cheeses and sliders help set the tone for a night of fun. You can tell your story by passing a mini version of the food you ate on your first date, food that speaks to either of your heritages, or items that are simply delicious. It's typical to select between four and ten passed items. Go for variety with meat, fish, and vegetarian items to keep all guests happy. Also try to have a mixture of fried versus fresh and hot versus cold, and look for an assortment of colors.

If you go for passed appetizers, look out for food that will be too messy for your guests, and know that items served on skewers or in shot glasses require the waitstaff to be extremely on top of their bussing game to keep the space clean. Stations allow you to serve items not suited for passing, and they can be great conversation pieces at cocktail hour. You can lean into being bougie and have caviar or a raw bar complete with oysters and lobster; keep it farm to table with a colorful grazing station of meat, cheese, and crudités; or go for something more creative. I've seen stations where you can select your favorite fillings for ramen served in a mug, a variety of dumpling trucks, stands with fries and dipping sauces, and a slew of other kitschy ones guests love.

There are some important rules that come along with choosing the food for cocktail hour:

- Don't overdo it! It is, by definition, only an hour.
- Guests should be able to consume passed appetizers in one bite.

THE CONCESSIONS

- Appetizers should whet the palate, not ruin appetites for the meal that follows.
- Be sure to consider the space you have available. Stations take up room, but self-service ones allow guests to access food without waiting for a server to come up to them. If the space is tight, it's better just to have passed items.
- If you have an overwhelmingly long list of options to choose from, wait until you select the actual meal so you can avoid repeating any.

JMK TIP

Have the cocktail party be your wedding reception. A cocktail party, which is different from a cocktail-style event, can save you money. Think of this more as something greater than a cocktail hour but not a full reception. This means you won't be serving a full meal, so it's less time you'll need to rent your venue, have a bar open, and pay vendors hourly. If you're opting for a cocktail party, be sure to advertise this so that guests aren't expecting a full meal. An invitation can read something like "Cocktails and canapés to follow." Make sure you have some seating available for guests, and don't forget that you'll still need to give structure to the timeline regardless of whether there will be a formal time for the meal.

■ BUFFET

Buffets are a great option if that's your preferred style of food service, but not for budgetary reasons. They're not only pricey but can often be more expensive than other options. When serving a plated meal, the kitchen staff controls the portions of each item being served. But when preparing a buffet meal, the kitchen staff must prepare for guests who'll take too much of one item, making sure it doesn't run out for others, and this extra food can run up the cost. That's not to say a fabulous buffet is anything less than fabulous.

Even though buffets are considered self-serve, you should always have staff manning them. They help quicken the line, assist your guests, and keep a handle on portion control. Buffets are also best suited to one-course meals. If you're having a three-course meal, try to serve the main course only at the buffet and reserve the salad and dessert courses for passing or plating. That way, guests don't have to go to the line more than once for their mains. Also, even though buffets technically differ from stations, which we'll get to later in this list, I still call a buffet a station because it makes it sound less like something you're lining up for on a cruise ship!

■ **COCKTAIL STYLE**

Cocktail-style meals allow you to provide your guests with a full dinner but not necessarily have them all sit at the same time. The first time I went to a wedding in New Orleans, I learned this is the only way to do a wedding there. The more of these I planned, the more I realized just how popular they are for certain crowds. Food can be served in a combination of ways, from passed items to different stations. Though there are some tables for guests, there's often more bar- or lounge-like furniture. Guests eat what they want, where they want, when they want. This usually allows more time for the party at the reception because you don't have to take the time to have all guests sit at the same time for meal service.

■ **FAMILY STYLE**

Family style is a less formal way of dining but wonderful for people like me who enjoy trying everything. With

THE CONCESSIONS

family-style meals, each guest has a plate in front of them, and the various foods are served on platters at each table for everyone to help themselves, much like the way we serve meals at home. There's beauty and casualness in guests passing dishes to each other, and if the food is noteworthy, it usually becomes a conversation topic. Consider family style only if that's the vibe you want, not as a way to save. The portions are usually robust, and they require much more serving equipment, so the rentals are usually higher. It's also important to take note of what tabletop décor you've planned. If you've spent a lot of money on centerpieces, you might be annoyed when staff has to remove them to accommodate a lot of platters.

■ FOOD TRUCKS

Food trucks are exactly what they sound like, but I have to say that if you're okay with this format, it's one of the most cost-effective ways you can feed your guests, and with very fresh food. If you dream of everyone sitting down at gorgeous table settings, this is not for you. But if the casualness doesn't bother you or if this attracts you, I'm here to tell you that some of my most buzzed-about weddings are ones that had food trucks. If you're pursuing this, I do recommend having something else alongside the trucks that's ready to go so guests can avoid having to wait in line for too long. This can be a table with chips, guacamole, and churros if you have a taco truck, or it can be salads, cheese and cured meats to accompany a pizza truck.

■ FRENCH SERVICE

If you're looking for the food service to be part of the entertainment—and if you're prepared for a high price tag—then French service might be for you. To this day, I've never seen this at a wedding, but as an author of due diligence I'm giving you a complete list. Servers come out with trolleys or large platters and prepare part of the meal tableside before serving it to the guests. This can be very time-consuming and requires highly proficient staff.

■ PLATED

Plated meals are like those at a restaurant: Each plate arrives for guests the way the chef designed it. Some couples consider this a necessity for any formal occasion, but I, of course, say you can make the call. When you arrange a plated meal with your caterer, you must decide whether you want your guests to have an option for their main course. You can choose one dish for everyone, and most places will offer a silent vegetarian option for guests who don't eat what you've selected, or you can let your guests choose what they'd like from two to three dishes (or more if you have a very small guest count).

One way you can often save a little money here is by having your guests preselect their choices when they RSVP. When I was first getting started as a planner in New York, preselecting was considered tacky. Many venues and guests would advocate for being able to experience reading a menu on the night of and then deciding based on mood. I agree that feels the most like a fine dining experience. However, preselecting can be a wonderful way to shave time off the food service, which you can use for more party time. It can be time-consuming for servers to get the orders of every table, and once they do, the chef finally learns how much of each dish they must make, so preselecting helps the staff be more prepared. Another option is to serve a duet—not of two pop divas but of food—such as a plate with a piece of steak and some fish.

■ RUSSIAN SERVICE

The price, timing, and staffing of Russian service is comparable to French service (also in that I've still never witnessed it). The food is made in the kitchen, and servers approach each guest and offer them whatever is on the platter they're holding. If this is appealing to you, know the time it will take to have every guest served, and remember there's always a chance even the most skilled server can spill sauce on a guest.

■ STATIONS

Stations differ from buffets in that they usually specialize in one type of food or cuisine. I've seen amazing paella stations and grazed at delicious carving stations. What's nice about a stationed dinner is the variety you can create for guests. I've done several weddings in New York where we brought in food from a few of the couple's favorite restaurants rather than creating stations through a caterer.

SETTLING ON THE MENU

Now that you know the ABCs of food service options, it's time to make your selections. There are some general guidelines you need to consider while doing this:

■ Taste It!

All venues and caterers should be able to provide a tasting in some capacity. Some strictly don't, and if that's their rule, you have to be okay with that. Be aware of their policies—some might ask you to come while they're preparing for another event, so you might not be able to taste everything you want to serve, and they might charge you if you bring guests to the tasting. Some even charge for the couple! Other venues offer a tasting as more of an open house where they invite several contracted couples. This can be a fun experience, but it might not be a chance to really discuss the food. I do believe in respecting chefs and their creations, but this is also *your* wedding. Be sure to schedule a tasting so you can make any changes you feel are necessary. There are plenty of restaurants where the menu sounds amazing, but when the food comes it's a major disappointment. That's not what you want at your wedding. Be sure you understand and are comfortable with the tasting policy before signing a contract!

■ View It!

Presentation is key, so really observe the food and the way it's served at your tasting, and ask how it will be presented. There's a caterer I've worked with multiple times who loves garnishing food with edible flowers. Some of my clients thought it was stunning, while others found it to be overkill. This is where your opinion really matters when discussing how they'll get the food to the table for your guest count, as preparing the food for your tasting is usually a much smaller feat than it will be at your wedding. Hopefully the food will either be covered with a "pretty hat," a catering term for the lid that keeps the food warm, or come directly from the kitchen if the distance is short enough to keep the food hot. But as Joanne from the musical *Company* might ask, "Does anyone still wear a hat?"

■ Trust It!

Work *with* your caterer, not against them. If you've booked a reputable venue or catering company, be sure to listen to their staff's advice. You should feel free to ask for custom items and critique during the tasting, but if they advise against something you want, trust them. Forcing a skilled Italian chef to make your favorite sushi dish might not work out. I once attended a tasting where the food was so bland we thought it wasn't finished. After we asked, we were told they usually prepare things that way to not offend out-of-towners with a less sophisticated palate. We pushed them to add more seasoning and spice to make the food more exciting, and my clients were much happier with the end

THE CONCESSIONS

result. In a situation like that, the chef is usually accommodating. Any caterer should be open to your feedback, just know that they might not be able to meet every request you have and that sometimes they know better.

■ Digest It!

Think about the food you want to serve and how it goes down. You don't want everyone feeling bloated or too heavy, or the dancing that's meant to follow might not happen!

■ Date It!

Think about the time of year and serve items that suit the season and accompanying temperature. A shot of gazpacho is for the summer, while French onion is for the winter!

■ Staff It!

Inquire about staff. Ask how many servers, bartenders, and captains you'll have (and no, the latter aren't pirates telling you what to do but the leads of the line staff). Pars for staff vary a bit from place to place, but generally for a seated dinner you want about one server per every ten guests, and for passed items it's about one server per every twenty-five guests. In theory, venues and caterers should be suggesting staffing that will make the service smooth and amazing, but everyone has a different standard here. Also find out what the staff will be wearing. If the uniform looks tacky, ask for other options. Requesting all black is usually a safe bet. Don't get too invested in the physical looks of the waitstaff though. There are companies that specialize in model-looking staff, but they aren't always the best at the job, and this isn't the time for you to feel intimidated by the hot bartender!

■ Time It!

Go over the timeline with your caterer or venue for each part of the food service and get a solid understanding of how long it will take them to serve your guest count. I've had many experiences when there was a moment I needed to cue after everyone was served, and watching how slowly the food was coming out of the kitchen was like watching paint dry. Guests shouldn't feel rushed, but each course should be no more than thirty minutes, including serving, dining, and clearing.

THE CAKE

Wedding cakes are as traditional to weddings as a woman in a white dress. But as you've learned, there's no rule saying you must keep any traditions. I've planned weddings with cakes so impressive they've been on the Food Network and others where we had no cake at all. If the two of you aren't into cake, this is a place you can save and go with whatever you want for dessert.

If you do want a cake, know that they usually cost more than you might think. You'll also need to find one that suits your style and delights your taste buds. Many bakers and pastry chefs solely make wedding cakes, and collaborating with you on the design is part of their process. One time, I planned a sci-fi-inspired wedding at a Waldorf Astoria that had a renowned French pastry chef. My clients wanted a cake in the shape of a dragon, with the intention of sabering off its head at the time of cake cutting. When we first shared this vision with the pastry chef, we thought he was going to throw his clipboard down and storm out. Instead, in a beautiful French accent he said, "Let me see what I can do." He then sketched out the vision and on the day of executed it perfectly, which thrilled my clients. Now, had he not been open to this, my clients could've told the venue they'd skip using their baker's cake and outsource the task to a baker who could handle it, so find out whether your caterer or venue does cakes; if not, you'll need to hire a separate vendor. As with all the other food, schedule an opportunity to taste it in advance.

Whichever way you go, be sure you trust who you're working with and follow some friendly cake guidelines:

THE CONCESSIONS

- **Give Inspiration**

  Begin by telling your baker your vision of the whole event, including the style, tone, and colors of your wedding and the story you're celebrating. See what ideas they come up with for you.

- **Get Personal**

  If one of you has a favorite type of cake, request that as the starting point. Can't decide on just one? The cake can alternate with each tier, and guests can pick their favorite. I've seen combinations such as red velvet and chocolate hazelnut.

- **Review the Concept**

  See a sketch of the design in advance. If you're going for a wedding cake, the design is equally important as the taste. Give your baker or caterer specifics of what you don't want, such as flowers made of icing.

- **Top with Detail**

  Everyone's entitled to their opinions here. Some couples adore having figurines of the two of them, while others roll their eyes at the mere thought. You can also use other objects that represent your personality, such as mini versions of your pampered pets, or you can have your initials monogrammed in frosting. Just remember that some things, like models, look better topless!

- **Control the Portions**

  Do you ever feel at weddings you have no room for a slice of the cake when it's served? You can have the cake sliced into small, bite-size pieces that servers can pass throughout the party. This saves not only some calories for your guests but also your money because you'll need less cake.

■ **Fake Out**
Have a really cool design concept for which it might be challenging to execute the edibility? Have a fake cake. Many bakers are proficient at the craft of creating something that looks real but is really just for show. Typically there's one slice built into it for you to do your ceremonial cut, but the rest is really arts and crafts while the kitchen has several sheet cakes to slice and serve to guests.

■ **Let Them Eat Cake (Again!)**
Themed takeaway boxes available at the cake table are wonderful gifts for your guests to take home. You can include a small note that they might not even discover until later. You can be sentimental, sarcastic, or even judgmental that they're having cake for breakfast!

■ **Freeze the Memory**
The tradition is to box up the top tier of your cake, put it in your freezer, and consume it when you celebrate your one-year anniversary. If you'd like to practice this tradition, be sure to arrange for the appropriate boxes in advance—and have room in your freezer. As an alternative, many bakers offer a mini version of a couple's cake that they can make fresh on the first anniversary.

JMK TIPS

Don't Be a Size Queen

If you want to have a cake-cutting moment without having a large-scale wedding cake, you can still slice into a regular-sized cake and serve other desserts to your guests. This can keep costs down and allow you to slice into something that might be from a bakery you really love.

THE CONCESSIONS

> **Don't Customize**
> Another way to save is by avoiding having a cake that's highly customized. Many bakeries offer certain cakes you can order online, and some are very bespoke. We've organized more than one exploding rainbow cake that still made a wow of this moment without breaking the bank!

SUGAR, BUTTER, FLOUR

Whether you're having a cake or not, dessert is meant to be a course that's indulgent, fun, and even a bit sinful. It's a wonderful chance to really use your creativity or, my favorite, incorporate more alcohol. Mini espresso martini shots and boozy milkshakes are always crowd favorites. Dessert is also another area where you can honor cultural or family traditions. If your budget allows, having desserts passed or at a station gives your guests a good excuse to get up rather than slip into a food coma at the table. You could also have a buffet of all your hometown's favorite treats, a themed station, a bar serving candy in your wedding colors, or a gelato cart with your favorite toppings, or you could play to your inner child and have cotton candy and funnel cakes. And yes, you can also cater to good health by having some fresh fruit.

LATE-NIGHT BITES

It has become increasingly popular to serve an extra round of savory food toward the last hour of the reception, especially if your guests might need something fried to counterbalance their drinking. I once overheard a guest say, "That slider is what saved me!" Late-night bites are definitely not the time to be health conscious, and they're ideal for bringing in your favorite indulgence that might not fit elsewhere in the menu or programming. You can arrange this through your caterer or venue, or you could bring something in from an outside source. One JMK couple who married at a St. Regis was obsessed with McDonald's chicken nuggets and fries, so both were passed around the dance floor while servers carried around all the dipping sauces on silver trays. We've also had In-N-Out trucks, Taco Bell buffets, and every kind of pizza imaginable.

BEVERAGES

I've said so many times when I'm asked to attend a wedding just as a guest, "You had me at open bar." The beverage menu is as important as the food menu, and it serves as another opportunity to share your story with your guests. It can also send your budget into the stratosphere, so let's break down the different stages of your event, each with some friendly JMK Tips that can help you save, because I say bottoms up!

■ GUEST ARRIVAL

It has become increasingly popular at weddings to serve guests drinks immediately upon their arrival. If you want your guests to arrive and be served knowing that several hours of drinking have begun, I recommend keeping things simple. Unless your event begins with cocktail hour, I recommend keeping pre-ceremony drinks to items passed on trays, such as champagne and sparkling water. At one wedding I planned, the couple told me champagne wasn't their thing, but a tequila and soda was, so that was their arrival drink. Think about whether you want guests to keep their drinks during the ceremony or you'd like staff to collect the glasses before guests take their seats. Remember: Your guests won't have anywhere to rest their glasses during the ceremony other than the floor, and the only glass broken during a ceremony should be by honoring the Jewish tradition. Also, if you're having an outdoor wedding or just something during a hot time of year, it's nice to greet your guests with a beverage that allows them to hydrate and cool down. Conversely, if it might be a bit chilly, it's nice to warm them up with a hot beverage.

JMK TIP

If you're interested in providing water, then spice it up. Have a few different beverage dispensers infused with colorful additions, such as cucumber, mint, oranges, or pineapple. It's visually appealing, will hydrate your guests before the drinking that follows, and shouldn't cost you more than a piece of fruit!

▪ COCKTAIL HOUR

Besides being a beloved time of any day, cocktail hour is many guests' favorite time at a wedding. You get to mingle, graze on appetizers, and, most importantly, enjoy the bar offerings. Besides making sure there's music, seating options for guests, and a few yummy nibbles, there are some other requirements for a successful cocktail hour:

- **Offer Tray-Pass Drinks**

    Always arrange to have guests greeted by servers with a small selection of drinks. There's nothing worse than starting a party by waiting in line with a hundred people at a bar.

- **Have at Least One Signature Drink or Specialty Cocktail**

    You can have trays of the drink you had on your first date, cocktails from your cultural heritage, or simply your two favorite things to drink. For a couple who met on a dating app, we featured the "Tinderita" and the "Swipe Right." This is also a wonderful place to incorporate your pets! Put their names in front of words such as "fizz" or "tini," and you've accomplished some branding. Again, think about the time of year here. An Aperol Spritz is more suited for the summer, while a Manhattan is better in winter. It's also important to provide your guests who don't imbibe with an interesting mocktail.

- **The Bar Should Be Far**

If there's flexibility in your floor plan, opt for the bar to be as far away from the entry as possible. This helps avoid a bottleneck when guests draw into the space.

- **Check the Staffing Standards**

Find out how many bartenders the venue plans on having. In the beginning of an event, I recommend having one bartender per fifty guests. If you're serving labor-intensive specialty cocktails, see whether they can pre-batch them to save time.

- **Don't Overdo It**

Have you ever felt overwhelmed by choices from a bar menu? You don't want to be standing behind that person at a wedding, so limit your offerings. It's perfectly acceptable to have one brand of each spirit you want to offer.

If it's in your budget and space allows, add some additional flair to the cocktail hour by having specialty bars. You can have a martini bar, a wine-tasting table, a spritz station, or a Bloody Mary bar with an assortment of ingredients and garnishes if it's an afternoon hour.

THE CONCESSIONS

As for budgeting, it's important to understand which bar packages are available and within your means. An "open bar" means you pay a flat rate for drinks to be unlimited, and a "consumption bar" means you pay per drink or bottle that's consumed. Usually the latter can be offered only at a venue that has a bar program. Sometimes a tab can be less expensive than the flat rate, but the downside to consumption bars is that you have no idea what you'll be paying for. In this case, you can arrange for management to notify you when the bill begins to near a given figure.

Sometimes there's an opportunity for you as the host to provide the products for the bar. A place that has a liquor license or requires a caterer to provide one won't be able to consider this, but a venue without those rules can work with you and your caterer to provide suggested quantities of the various wine and spirits you'll need. This gives you an opportunity to organize exactly what you want, shop for sales, and usually even keep the leftovers. The only downside can be figuring out the logistics of buying and then transporting the items.

JMK TIP

If you're having a consumption bar, don't be afraid to limit what the bar can offer to keep the costs more reasonable. You don't necessarily need to have shots of top-shelf tequila available.

If you know your crowd will be drinking all night, try to go with an open bar. Another option is to have an open bar just during cocktail hour, then limit the selection to wine and beer during the reception.

JMK TIP

While an open bar is valuable to guests who drink, see whether you can negotiate to avoid paying for your non-drinking guests, such as the underaged, the pregnant, and the recovering. Usually there's a cheaper refreshment option for them.

With either an open bar or a consumption bar, find out which tier of spirits will be included. Most places have a standard package with house spirits and the option to upgrade to premium or top shelf.

JMK TIP

While I'm someone who loves a good brand name, most people don't pay close attention to the bottles being used behind a bar at a wedding. As long as you're not serving boxed wine, the standard package might be fine and a good way to control costs.

Be sure to analyze all prices to keep your beverages in line with your budget. Even if you're starting to feel overwhelmed by numbers, do *not* contemplate a cash bar. Guests should not be paying for anything at your wedding unless they just discovered your registry and are making a gift happen in real time.

THE CONCESSIONS

JMK TIP

Other than a particularly sassy friend, guests won't complain about what's being offered. Champagne is usually an add-on to bar packages, and while many associate bubbly with weddings, it's okay to forgo it to save. It's also fine to serve only wine and beer, and that's always a considerable savings from having spirits.

■ **THE RECEPTION**

Once your guests finish cocktail hour, it's time to transition them to the main event. Unless you're having a cocktail-style wedding, at some point your guests will sit to eat and the wine will be poured. Most bar packages include some type of house wine for this. Some venues have delicious house wines, while others include very cheap wine to entice you to upgrade. I recommend tasting the wine that's included and making sure you're happy with it. If you drink only vodka and have no palate for wine, bring a friend who's a wine connoisseur and can advise you. If you're underwhelmed with the included wine, you may be able to negotiate a different variety at the same price point. Also find out whether the wine that's included will be poured tableside and, if so, whether the venue charges extra for that.

JMK TIP

If you really want to go above and beyond what's offered with wine, see whether you can bring in your own. While a venue will charge you a corkage fee, this is a way you can offer better quality products for less money.

Find out what the sparkling option is. Technically, champagne is only Champagne if it's from the Champagne region, which is often the most expensive. If you can't afford to have it, you can opt for a delicious sparkling wine from another region, such as Prosecco or Cava. If what's included in the package isn't the best glass of bubbly you've had, try turning it into a type of champagne cocktail.

JMK TIP

Skip the champagne toast and just have everyone raise their glasses with whatever they're drinking.

Don't get too caught up in the wine and champagne offerings, especially since most guests will never notice the bottles anyway.

JMK TIP

If you've arranged for a tab at a consumption bar, discuss drink service with the catering manager. Ask for wine to be refilled only upon request and for glasses to be cleared only if they're empty.

You guessed it. It's time to return to the workbook and put everything in one place. Scroll over to the Menu Planning Worksheet and fill it in with all the information you've collected about your menu, your cake, and your beverage offerings. Here's an example:

THE CONCESSIONS

FOOD

Guest Arrival
N/A

Cocktail Hour

Passed
Caviar Potato Chips, Mini Reubens, Truffle Arancini
Crispy Rice Tuna, Eggplant Parm Bite, Hamachi Taquito

Stationery
Grazing Table, Raw Bar

First Course

Plated
Arugula, Shaved Artichoke, Avocado, Parmesan Shards, Vinaigrette

Main Course

Family Style
Filet Mignon, Chimichurri, Rosemary Roasted Potatoes
Roasted Halibut, Snow Peas, Black Rice
Mushroom Risotto

Desert

Passed
Tiramisu Cream Puffs, Nutella Donuts, Red Velvet Ice Cream Sandwiches

Late Night
Assorted Sliders & Fries

BEVERAGE

Guest Arrival
Passed Aperol Spritz, Mock Spritz, Sparkling Water

Cocktail Hour

Specialty Cocktails
Mezcal Negroni, Smoked Old Fashioned, Pineapple Mocktail
Premium Open Bar

Dinner
Upgraded Wines: Sancerre & Petite Syrah

Dessert
Passed Espresso Martinis

Additionally, add to your Run of Show what you've arranged in terms of food service, such as when the first course will be served or a dessert station will open. Once you're set on what traditions and musical or other moments you want, the order of certain dances and toasts, the caterer needs to review this document to establish how much time they'll have between them. If your venue needs only fifteen minutes to clear the first course and bring out the main, it might be the perfect time for a toast. If they need longer, it might be more ideal for a family dance that gradually invites all your guests up to dance until the next course is ready.

Do you feel ready to eat, drink, and be married? If so, get ready to create an environment that sets the mood in which your guests can enjoy the delicious menu.

ENDNOTE

1. Oscar Wilde, *A Woman of No Importance* (Penguin Books, 1996), act 2.

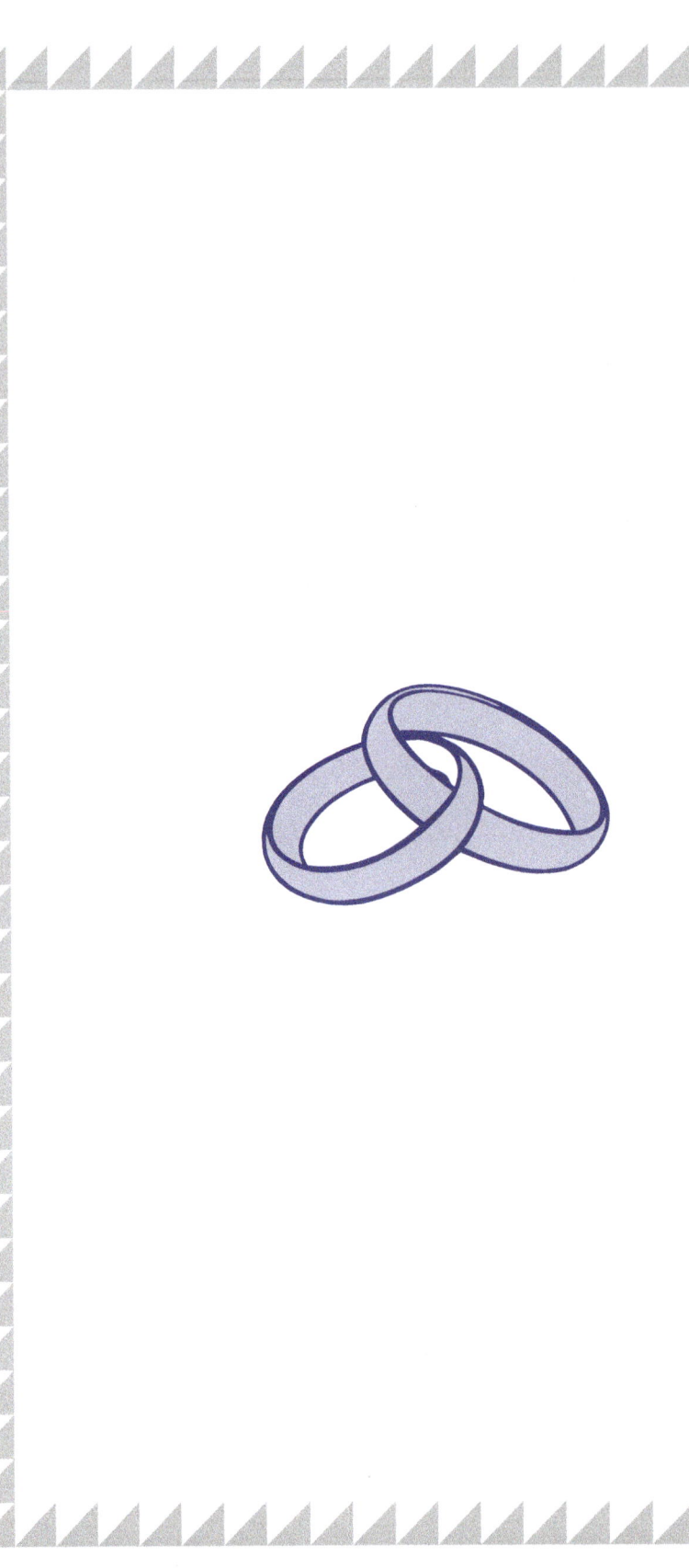

Chapter 9

SET DESIGN

For years the incomparable Bette Midler has sung about love being a flower and the lovers its only seed. I wanted to mention her for multiple reasons:

- In case you had any doubts until now, here's where I tell you that, yes, I'm that gay!
- She's been my absolute favorite diva since I was a child, and I've never wavered on her being my number one.
- I think *Big Business* is the most fantastic comedy of all time and is my go-to movie whenever I need a pick-me-up or just a good laugh.
- I grew up on her performance as Mama Rose in the made-for-television movie *Gypsy*, and despite all the live revivals I've adored since, hers is still my favorite.
- The revival of *Hello Dolly* she headlined, and all seven times I saw it, are some of my happiest memories in the theater. (My dog is also named Barnaby, if you doubt my commitment.)

Now that I've likely lost the handful of straight men who were reading this book, let's get Bette to business!

Now, I'm a wedding planner, not a lyricist, but I say, "love is a flower—or any other visual touch—and you its only designing seeds." If you recall Midler as Janis Joplin in the film *The Rose*, the sheer gift that there's not one but two characters named Rose in *Big Business*, and the way she incorporates her signature walk and shimmy into the song "Rose's Turn," you might want to imagine only roses at your wedding. Listen, I hear you. Maybe you never want to picture this object of nature, or any flower, as a design element of your wedding, and perhaps I'm the first wedding planner to tell you that's perfectly acceptable. It's your day. The only requirement for the visual design of your event is to put as much thought into it as every other element.

The design layout of your event can have such a powerful effect on you and your guests. It can remind people to appreciate the beauty in the existing surroundings, and it can take everyone into your version of a dream-like wonderland. For many couples, this (and the food) is the most fun part of the entire wedding planning process. With creativity, imagination, and personalization, you can create a fabulous experience regardless of how much you've allotted for visuals in your budget.

To turn fantasy into reality, you must determine two things: (1) What does the set design of your show look like? and (2) Are you able to achieve this on your own, or do you need to employ some help? There's a slew of professionals who can help in this department, including those we're about to discuss. I realize some of you might live in a space you designed completely on your own that could be featured in *Architectural Digest*, but others might need a little help, so let's start with the pros.

THE PROS

Even if you have a very clear picture of what you want your set to look like, you'll need some key players to execute it on the day of.

SET DESIGN

Despite whether you went into this knowing the dream look of your set design, it's not like you're intending to execute it yourself on the day of.

▪ DRAPERS

Some spaces are truly enhanced by draping, whether it's to hide a certain space until it's ready to be revealed, create hallways where they don't exist structurally, or shrink a space that might be too big. Sometimes draping is simply decorative and can soften a ceiling or draw attention to it by highlighting its grandeur. Many rental companies offer to drop off a simple pipe-and-drape setup, but for anything a bit more complex, you'll need a company that specializes in drapery.

▪ EVENT DESIGNERS

Whether you're working with a planner or not, you might want to hire a designer. They can be especially helpful if your vision requires multiple components to come to life and each comes from a different source. They sometimes work with wedding planners who are responsible for executing the vision on-site, while others handle that themselves.

▪ EVENT PLANNERS

Some of us planners can also handle the design, from the creative ideation to the on-site execution. If you're working with someone who does it all, that might be sufficient, or if nothing else, they'll likely be very clear about others you need to hire for your production team.

▪ FLORISTS & FLORAL DESIGNERS

At the risk of sounding obvious, florists and floral designers specialize in the floral aspect of your wedding. Some draw strict rules and say it's the only element they get involved in, while others weigh in on all other aspects of design, such as rental furniture and tabletop items. As you interview them, be sure to understand the scope of their work. We'll dive deeper into this in the next chapter.

■ Lighting Designers

Some weddings can be beautifully achieved using existing in-house lighting on dimmers and candles, while others require being lit like a full production. Depending on how elaborate your lighting desires are, you might want someone who specializes in this. Sometimes your planner or event designer will handle this simply by securing the equipment needed from an AV company.

■ Rental Companies

You'll usually need to rent any item that's a part of your vision but isn't provided by your venue. For the record, I've had clients who chose to purchase items in bulk when they found the prices comparable, but not all of us have a need to own 150 gold chargers for future entertaining purposes. Some rental companies are large and carry every type of item you may need, while others have a niche, such as carrying only specialty linen. Some rental items you might need to factor into your décor include furniture, linen, flooring, candles, additional lighting, and tabletop items.

As you might be able to tell from this breakdown, and like most everything else we've discussed, your set design team is not a one-size-fits-all. There's a lot of crossover in the industry regarding who does what. I've planned weddings with floral installations at venues that didn't allow items to be hung from the ceiling, so we had to work with an AV company to bring in trusses that created an area for the flowers to be hung, then we draped the poles to hide them. It's truly a team effort.

As you pursue hiring some of these pros, you should already have a good understanding of the venue you've chosen. Is it a place so beautiful and rich in character and scene that it needs very little, or do you need to completely transform the space? During the work we did together in previous chapters, what story did you decide to tell your guests? Is it an old-fashioned love classic under the stars, a campy romp with humor and drama, or a modern, sleek, and sophisticated story? Is it a mystery, comedy, or a little bit of both? Do you want your ceremony and reception to feel like two different places, even if they're in the same location? Let's break this down by starting with the big picture, then we'll gussy it up. As we go through this, begin saving images online that inspire you. You can use Pinterest, create a photo album, or any other system you like.

SCENE-BY-SCENE LAYOUT

It's important to walk through the guest experience of your set design from start to finish and identify how each area needs to be laid out. I recommend going through this chronologically because that's the way your crowd will experience it, but that's not to say it's in order of importance.

■ ENTRYWAY/PRE-EVENT

What's the first thing your guests will see when they enter? Maybe it's as simple as a sign that reads, "Welcome to Our Wedding." Maybe it's a staircase leading into a building that would be just a bit more magical if the railing were wrapped in greenery and had some tall pillar candles at its base. Do you want your event to feel like an opening night? Perhaps you need a red carpet with a step-and-repeat backdrop. I once planned a wedding on a rooftop in New York where guests had to enter through a dingy garage before getting to the elevator that took them upstairs. We learned that many other couples would line the walkway with candles to spruce it up a bit, but my clients decided it would be more fun to lean into the grit of it, making most guests wonder whether they were in the right spot for the wedding until the elevator opened up to the roof.

JMK TIPS

Check Storage Space

Unless your wedding is taking place somewhere or sometime when the weather is of no concern, don't forget to think about where people might check their coats or umbrellas!

Worried About Crashers?

I've definitely planned weddings where crashers arrived for a variety of reasons. If this is a concern or possibility, look into adding a security measure, such as collecting all RSVPs and generating a day-of guest list that can then be checked off as guests arrive. If your venue or catering staff won't oversee this, be sure to assign someone to manage it, as you certainly won't want to be dealing with party crashers during your wedding.

■ CEREMONY

After your guests have entered and taken their seats, what will be the backdrop for Act 1? The most traditional layout for a ceremony is having rows of chairs (as many as needed for your guest count) with an aisle down the middle. The back of the aisle is where the two of you and anyone else in the processional make their entrance. The front of the aisle after the first row of chairs leads to the ceremony space; in religious ceremonies, this would include either a chuppah, an altar, or a mandap that's often elevated.

However, when we broke down the traditions of wedding ceremonies, we established that there are no rules. That holds true here, especially if you're not physically bound by what your space allows. Nowhere does it say any of this is required. You can have a ceremony in the round,

SET DESIGN

or you could create a house that has two aisles allowing for staggered entrances. I once planned a wedding for a musician who organized an incredible rotation of performances throughout the ceremony and dinner. After we weighed the logistics of what was possible at the venue, we decided it made the most sense to begin with cocktail hour, have everyone seated at their tables for the ceremony, then commence with dinner and the show. At another ceremony I planned, we created one giant single-row spiral of chairs, and the couple loved how walking down the aisle that way allowed them to make eye contact with all two hundred guests before they arrived at the ceremony spot. I've also done weddings for couples who didn't want the ceremony to feel as much like a show, so we planned a casual gathering of people standing around in no pattern at all. What aligns most with your vision and is also feasible at your venue?

Sometimes the most breathtaking part of the design is where you two finally land for the ceremony. Remember: Whatever you select to serve as your backdrop will be in all your ceremony photos. I've mentioned some religious options, such as designing a chuppah for a Jewish ceremony or decorating an altar for a Christian one. For extra impact, I've planned weddings with automated floating chuppahs and altars that rose higher in the air as the couple kissed!

If formal or elaborate elements don't speak to you, I recommend at the very least trying to frame the two of you in some way. This can be something like adorning a canopy or arch or doing something a little less expected. Two freestanding pedestals with trees or plants can make a splash, but I think it's best when they're asymmetrical to add a bit of character. At one wedding I planned for two musicians, music is what brought them together, so we rented a hexagonal structure to go behind them and decorated it with flowers made from old sheet music. During the pandemic I worked with a couple who could no longer encourage their guests to travel to their wedding, so they asked all guests to mail them paper flowers and then incorporated them into the chuppah, which made it feel as though those guests were there physically. I've also seen guests simply root themselves under an existing beautiful tree and then surround the area where the couple stood with candles.

All weddings are beautiful in their own ways. It's up to you to determine what you want the ceremony and guest seating area to look and feel like for this aspect of your wedding.

JMK TIPS

Include Extra Chairs

Always have extra chairs for seating beyond your guest count. Some guests prefer a little distance from others, and they still deserve a seat!

Plan for the Weather

If you're having an outdoor wedding, you should already know the contingency plan for inclement weather, but also think about what might just be nice to offer your guests. For something in the heat and sun, have an entry table with bug spray, sunscreen, and parasols. For somewhere potentially chilly, have a table of pashminas or one waiting for every guest on their chairs.

■ COCKTAIL HOUR

Cocktail hour is only an hour, so if you're looking at areas where you can scale back on layout, this is the ideal time. Conversely, if you have a quirky idea you want to explore or a color you love that doesn't quite fit in with the rest of the wedding, this is an opportunity for something to be relatively stand-alone. An important aspect of cocktail hour is

SET DESIGN

that it's usually where guests learn where they'll be sitting afterward. For this component, your escort display can be as much of a design statement as your space allows. It's also important to have a mixture of furniture. Highboy or bar tables are great for guests who prefer to stand, but be sure to include some seating for guests who'd rather not. As you work on the floor plan for this part of the event, account for how many tables and surfaces will need to be decorated. Simple votive candles and bud vases can go a long way in making the space look inviting when guests first enter, and they're also practical because they don't take up too much real estate on tables your guests are using as they consume food and drink.

■ RECEPTION

Act 2 is your next opportunity for a big wow. It's wonderful if your wedding venue has three distinct spaces for the ceremony, the cocktail hour, and the reception, but don't be concerned if you learn "flipping the space" is required. A venue should advertise or suggest this only if they know it's possible, and having orchestrated it multiple times in my career, I know it just about always is. Sometimes even when we're at the fifty-seven-minute mark, we're still making sure chairs are perfectly aligned, candles are being lit, and the dance floor is getting one final sweep.

Regardless of whether this is all preset or not, you must agree to and sign off on the final floor plan. Hopefully by this point you understand your venue's level of flexibility, and for spaces where these elements aren't necessarily built in, you might have some exciting choices to make. I've created weddings for clients where all the tables surrounded the dance floor and others where the dining and dancing sections were totally separate. The design of your reception not only dictates the flow of your event but clarifies how many dining tables are needed, including their shapes and sizes. Even if you're having a cocktail-style wedding without any assigned seating, you still need to assess how many open-seating tables and lounge areas a venue has and what their design requirements are.

If you're not working with a pro here, a good place to start is by asking your venue for some sample floor plans suited to your guest count. Besides the seating, you'll also need to consider locations for the dance floor, the entertainment, bars, and any stations you're including.

FURNITURE

Your venue may or may not include furniture, and you may or not like it. This creates an opportunity to further enhance your set design.

■ TABLES

Event tables come in many shapes and materials besides the wooden or plastic folding ones you might be familiar with that require linen. While renting nicer wooden farm tables can sometimes be more expensive, they give that more rustic aesthetic many people prefer. For more modern designs, there are acrylic, lacquered, and mirrored tables that can make a huge impact. If something like this fits your vision, price this out to see what works best for your budget. Imagine an all-black table set with white china, and down the middle is an alternation of a single white bud and white candles. This would create drama without the cost of including centerpieces.

Table sizes and shapes have often caused debates among JMK clients, so let's look at the plaintiffs in each case:

- **Round v. Long**

  Advocates for round tables often prefer them because they allow you to see all the guests at the table, which they say makes for better conversation. However, when it comes to design, I find it's easier to make something more striking at long tables. And truthfully, even when I'm sitting at a round table, I find I converse only with the person to the left or right of me. When I'm at a long table, I chat with those next to me and the person across from me. But regardless of my case for why I like certain things long, it's essential you see the big picture of what works best at your venue.

What's most important for the event is an excellent traffic pattern that allows for good service and for guests not to feel trapped. Think about how your set would look from a bird's-eye view. I once created a wedding for two hundred guests who all sat at three long tables, just under seventy guests per table. The next time I worked at that same venue, I showed my new clients some photos of this, and they told me they thought it looked like the dining hall at Hogwarts, then opted for round tables. So, set design is subjective, but it's ultimately something you must plan.

JMK TIPS

Fill the Tables

Round tables tend to require more décor to feel full, while long ones have less distance between the guests and therefore need less.

Don't Obstruct!

Whether round or long, guests don't like having something blocking their view, especially right at eye level. While I love tall arrangements, if doing one, make sure they're above eye level and don't obstruct a guest's line of vision while seated.

● Head v. Sweetheart

We've made the case for your guests and what their conversations over dinner might be like, but how about the two of you? Deciding where you'll sit is another element you might have a gut instinct about, but you'll need to weigh the pros and cons for both personal and practical reasons. Many couples sit at a sweetheart table, which is a table just for the two of you that's typically in the center or in front of the guest tables. The pros to this scenario are not hurting anyone's feelings about who sits at your table, and you might get to enjoy a little time without having to make conversation with your guests. The cons to this scenario are putting your duo of a dining section on full display, and you might have guests constantly coming up to you who wouldn't if you were sitting with others.

JMK TIP

See if any of your ceremony décor can be repurposed for your sweetheart table. If you were framed during your vows, why not reuse that décor during your meal?

Your other option is a head table, which is a table you two share with your wedding party, family, or some combination of the two. Many wedding designs have guest tables at standard capacities, such as ten or twelve guests, but the head table can be much larger depending on how many people you'd like to include there. This is usually a better option for JMK couples who prefer to be more social over dinner.

SET DESIGN

JMK TIP

If you're seating guests on both sides of a long table, the two of you should be centered where most guests in the room have sight of you. Try putting at least two empty chairs directly across from you so that everyone has a better line of sight.

Once you've gotten a good sense of the floor plan you like, you'll be able to have a better idea of what you then need to make it come alive. Remember: You'll be able to make final adjustments once all your RSVPs are in.

■ CHAIRS

Your guests will be walking into a space where the tables and chairs are on full display, so be sure to choose something that complements your story. I once had a floral sample viewing at a venue where my clients couldn't put their finger on what they weren't liking. After the florist provided many suggestions for revision, my client finally realized it wasn't the flowers but the chairs; they couldn't get past the ones that had been set in front of them.

Many venues include Chiavaris, or ballroom chairs. They come in every color and are light and easy to move around. Chances are you've seen and used them multiple times, even if you didn't realize it at the time. Some venues simply don't upkeep their furniture, so it's essential to check the condition it's in. A banquet table with some dents in it will go unnoticed once it's dressed properly with linens and tabletop designs, while a busted chair will still be busted.

Have fun while you select chairs. There's no rule that says they all have to be identical. You can have a beautiful barn wedding with completely mismatched antique wooden chairs or a more modern interior with a color-blocked pattern by alternating chair types at different tables.

JMK TIPS

Low on Budget?
If you fall in love with a certain chair and table combination but simply can't afford it for your entire guest count, do it just for the head table.

Doing a Hora?
Be sure to think about which two chairs will be used. If the chairs you have for the ceremony or dining aren't safe to be lifted in, secure two that are.

■ Bars & DJ Booths

Besides what's needed for dining, there might be other places to consider bringing in some additional furniture. Ask your venue or caterer what they plan to set up for a bar. Often it's simply a folding table clothed in black. If you have a floor plan with a central bar, you can choose to make that the standout. At one wedding I planned, the only pieces we rented were to create one giant mirrored round bar in the center of the reception. You can also look to rental companies for more decorative DJ booths and stage fronts.

Don't forget to think about some lounge furniture. You'll need to map out what you have space for, but many JMK clients love when there's some type of breakout space from the dining tables or a place to rest near the dance floor for those who are more likely to watch. Materials such as velvet, suede, and leather can help warm up a space, and bold colors and patterns in a lounge can sometimes make a statement that would otherwise be too big if repeated at every guest setting.

FLOORING

Now that we've touched on what you and your guests will sit in, let's discuss what everyone will walk and dance on.

If you're having any kind of outdoor reception, it's imperative to at the very least rent a dance floor. If you're installing a tent and the grounds aren't particularly flat, you might want to consider flooring for the entire event. Trying to dine at a wobbly table isn't exactly a vibe most couples want to create!

If the event is indoors, that doesn't mean you can forget about the dance floor. Think about where you're expecting dancing to take place and what the surface of the floor is made of. If it's suitable for dancing you might be fine, but this also creates an opportunity for design. A black-and-white checkered dance floor or an LED one that changes colors to the beat of the music creates a more dramatic effect than an all-wood one. Conversely, a solid dance floor is a great place for adding a decal or reflecting some interesting lighting.

Many indoor spaces, such as those in hotels, are often carpeted. Though these venues might have a dance floor, most of the space will typically be carpeted in a pattern that makes you question who designed the space; I've seen *so* many JMK clients gasp at this. I don't know why these venues go with these designs rather than something more neutral, but I will tell you this: There's a decent chance that when you first view a space, it won't be lit the way it would be for your event, and if you do have to use a venue with carpeting, keep in mind that it will fade away once you transform the room with candles and an ambient amber glow.

One other piece of flooring you might want to consider is for the ceremony. Older traditions involved laying out an aisle runner right before the ceremony to mark the beginning of it. That might feel a little archaic to you, but if you're leaning into any old-timey or regal vibes, it might be the perfect way to set the tone. On a practical note, it can also even and soften the runway to allow greater ease of walking down it.

LIGHTING

Lighting might be the most underestimated and undervalued component of set design. No matter how beautiful or creative your vision turns out, your guests need to be able to see it. This is another area where, especially if you're attempting anything other than the bare minimum, I suggest bringing in a pro.

The first thing to assess is whether lighting comes with your venue and, if so, what its capabilities are. I once attended an event in a museum where the hosts hadn't considered this, so all they had for their event were fluorescent lights that couldn't be dimmed. The bright lights stayed on all night, and so did our sunglasses.

I'm a person who has dimmers on literally every light in my apartment, including my bathroom and closet (yes, I'm a little obsessed with lighting levels). This is far more important to consider for weddings than for my nightly at-home rituals! Ideally, your venue will have dimmable lighting that can change throughout the event as needed. A room with windows will be very different once the sun sets, and the vibe you're going for may drastically differ from the start of cocktail hour to the final dance. For some, dimmable in-house lights and candles are sufficient, but for those interested in something a bit more, here's some of the lighting lingo you can discuss with a pro.

- **AMBIENT LIGHTING**
    Ambient lighting is the light you see on the walls of event spaces, and it includes uplighting and downlighting. Not to sound too obvious, but uplighting rests on the ground and projects light up, while downlighting is just the opposite. To give lighting a hue, experts often use gels, which are filters that come in all colors and are placed in front of lights. Though ambient lighting can be in any color, it's especially nice in soft white or champagne. It's almost always included for the reception and often for cocktail hour and the ceremony.

SET DESIGN

■ CEILING TREATMENTS

Depending on your set design and venue, you could hang a ceiling treatment over the dance floor, such as disco balls, a chandelier, lanterns, Edison bulbs, café string lights, or custom floral designs. Your designer and florist will usually make these decisions with you, helping you choose something that's already available or working on a custom look. For the record, a disco ball with a light shining on it to create a fun effect has stood the test of time and is still used at weddings today. They range in size, and we've done massive installations of several disco balls hanging together.

■ GOBOS

A gobo is a design or pattern that's installed into a projection fixture to project an image of a specified size. For white light projection, they're made of steel, and for full-color projection they're made of glass. You can have a gobo designed with a personal touch, such as your logo, a special image, or a quote, and have it illuminated. If you want a custom image, you'll need to get the designer's approval prior to creation to ensure that when the image is projected onto a surface it's of high quality.

■ INTELLIGENT LIGHTING

Intelligent lighting is the kind that can move and project different colors and patterns, and it's often used to create cool effects on dance floors and stars on ceilings. The fixtures are controlled by a board, and the system can create both static projections for guest entry and high-energy projections as the party gets going. If this interests you, you'll need to hire a moving light programmer to control the system.

■ LED NEON

Besides creating a static sign, which you can do, LED neon is also used to enhance a party. This type of lighting can be adhered to or hung from surfaces such as entryways, hallways, stairways, or columns; used to create a border around a stage; or be hung as individual tubes. Unlike real neon lighting, LED neon is programmable so it can change color to the beat of the music, and it's not fragile like real neon, which can easily shatter.

■ PIN SPOTS

Pin-spot lighting comes from fixtures installed from above that focus beams of light down to highlight a specific area, such as dining tables and florals. It's a great way to make sure all the work that went into your floral and tabletop design is better appreciated. It also works well to highlight bars and food stations, and not just as functional lighting for those working them, but to beautifully highlight bottles and glassware and make food look more appetizing.

■ SPOTLIGHTS

Spotlights are like those in a theater's technical booth, and they're used to draw attention to special entertainment moments, such as the first dance. This is most often done in dimmable white light so that certain areas and the performers are properly lit throughout the event.

■ STRING LIGHTS

As the term implies, string lights are bulbs on strings (clever, I know), and they can be hung in a variety of patterns to create tremendous ambience. Sometimes referred to as "café string lights," they're standard-sized bulbs on strands that are draped from side to side or in a pattern to create a specific atmosphere. You also might hear this described as "string lights on dropdowns," which is when a grid is created for each bulb to be hung at a different height for a modern industrial effect. There's also "twinkle lights," a type of sting light used in trees or wrapped around columns, usually with a bulb size and shape associated with holiday décor.

■ TRUSS OR TREE

In the world of lighting, a truss tower or tree is the construction used to install lights from above so that they can shine down on an area. They're often used when a venue doesn't allow installation of fixtures from rig points in the ceiling.

■ WASHES

Wash lighting is similar to ambient lighting, but it's more of a general setting, usually an application of soft and unfocused colored light that gives ambience to an area or a room. At minimum, plan to provide a wash for the band or dance floor. There are also textured washes that use gobos to cascade patterns across various surfaces, including dance floors, table spaces, large decorative installations, and even walls and ceilings. Sometimes they're just texture, but they can be done with a more literal pattern, such as leaves on the ground.

Do you have a sense of the floor plans for each component of your event? Do you know what furniture and rentals you need to pull that off? Then guess what time it is. Yep! Visit the workbook and scroll over to the Rental Checklist. You should also continually add to wherever you are saving images that inspire you, and the Rental Checklist is where you start listing everything you need to bring in to pull that off. Here are some examples:

WE DO

RENTAL CHECKLIST

WHEN	ITEM	QTY	LINK
Ceremony			
	Chairs	200	
	Altar	1	
Cocktail Hour			
	Bars	2	
	Hi Cocktail Tables	4	
	Hi Table Linen	4	
	Low Cocktail Tables	4	
	Low Table Linen	4	
	Low Table Chairs	16	
	Food Station Tables	2	
	Station Linen	2	
	Sofas	2	
	Arm Chairs	4	
	Coffee Tables	2	
Reception			
	Dance Floor	1	
	Stage	1	
	Bars	2	
	Dining Tables	15	
	Table Linen	15	
	Dining Chairs	150	

SET DESIGN

Do you feel confident in the foundation for your set? Then let's move ahead to decorating it!

Scan to download the workbook.

Chapter 10

SET DECORATION & ACTIVATIONS

With a good sense of the overall set design of your event, it's time to move on to making it all the more special by decorating it! In the last chapter, we laid out the pros you need for design, and there is some crossover here. Let's begin by discussing what might be the most predictable element used in wedding design.

FLOWERS

Though flowers are probably the most expected part of wedding décor, if you don't want flowers at all, I'm here to tell you that I've done plenty of weddings without them, so you can skip this section if you'd rather.

For those of you who are still here, I need to tell you that this section is challenging to explain without attaching some gender norms to it, as that's where many of these traditions came from. But I've had grooms carry bouquets and brides wear boutonnieres, so as with everything else, you do you! This section also isn't intended to make you a floral expert; we're not going to get into flower varieties and what time of year they're most in bloom. If that's of interest to you, there are many resources you can use to learn. Besides reading books and internet articles, I recommend discussing this with a florist.

Other than in a handful of circumstances, I do not recommend taking on flowers as a DIY project. To give you some context, I once planned a wedding in the desert with a highly organized and design-minded groom. He wanted only succulents and to plant them only in sand-filled glass cylinders alternating between pillar candles. We did the math to determine how many he needed per table, ordered all the necessary components, and organized an assembly party just days before the wedding. This worked because succulents aren't finicky like many flowers; they can withstand handling by nonprofessionals and don't require watering and trimming. For a different wedding, a mom arranged flowers as a hobby and wanted to offer them to guests as gifts. After discussing with my client whether this would prevent his mom from enjoying herself or achieving the vision he wanted, the answer to both was no. The mom really wanted to assemble the centerpieces, so that's what she did.

In the second case, my client really didn't care what the flower arrangements would look like, but most of my clients are more particular, so a professional is the way to go. When you first meet with them, go over the vision you first identified for the wedding. Think of this as a collaboration. Ideally, the florist should inspire you and help strengthen your ideas while also understanding your budget. If you don't feel that way about a particular florist, perhaps they're not the right vendor for you.

When considering the floral design of your wedding, keep these details in mind for each event space:

- **CEREMONY**

    In addition to the actual ceremony space that frames you, flower arrangements can be included at entryways,

SET DECORATION & ACTIVATIONS

especially if they have tables of yarmulkes and/or programs. You can also use them to line the aisle as well as to frame the back of it where you'll enter, and vines are great for wrapping industrial columns or treating ceilings.

- **COCKTAIL HOUR**

For cocktail hour, flowers should be placed on all guest tables, including highboy tables, low-rise cocktail tables, and coffee tables. They should also decorate bars and food stations as well as the escort display and any other display table, such for the guest book or gifts.

- **RECEPTION**

At the reception, be sure to place flowers at all guest tables, including those for dining and those for lounging. They're also nice for decorating the bar, display tables, food stations, the cake table, and any favor displays. You can also add flowers to a chandelier above the dance floor or use them to frame the entertainment, and trees are great for marking the four corners of the dance floor. Go with whatever creations bring your vision to life.

- **PERSONALS**

If you're someone who identifies as a bride and finding the perfect dress is one of your top priorities, chances are the bouquet you'll be holding is as crucial as any other accessory. As you discuss this design with your florist, be sure to review how it will compliment your dress. Besides the type of flowers used, you'll want to consider size and scale. A bouquet is also a fantastic place to incorporate something sentimental you want close to you on your wedding day, such as a family heirloom. For the record, one of my most famous brides simply wasn't the bouquet type, so she opted to wear a crown of flowers, which was more fitting for her.

Whether there's no bride in your wedding or you're like my aforementioned client, there are additional personals to consider. If there will be other women walking down the aisle, it's fairly standard to provide them with either corsages or smaller bouquets that are similar in style to the bride's but smaller in scale. I once worked with two grooms who didn't carry bouquets but had their best ladies carry them in all the colors of the rainbow! Mothers and any other female family members are usually provided a bouquet or corsage. If that sounds too prom-inspired, there are many more modern designs to choose, such as floral bracelets. People wearing a suit, tuxedo, or outfit with a jacket of any kind are usually adorned with a boutonniere. These are typically made for the groom or grooms, but they can also be worn by others walking down the aisle who aren't carrying bouquets.

Keep in mind that personals can be messy. I once worked with two grooms who bought brand-new white Tom Ford tuxes and did not want to risk anything staining them, so they went without personals. As a specialist in nontraditional weddings, I find it so beautiful to let personal flowers really enhance the individual types of people my clients have chosen to be in their party.

JMK TIPS

Repurpose Handheld Flowers

For any handheld flowers, be sure you have a plan for them after the ceremony. They can be repurposed into design, or you could have empty vases waiting for them in a suite. If you'd like those who'll be carrying them during the ceremony to enjoy cocktail hour afterward, they'll need their hands free.

SET DECORATION & ACTIVATIONS

Preserve the Bouquet
If you're carrying a bouquet you'd like to preserve, be sure to prearrange this. There are all sorts of companies that can frame them once dried or turn them into art. If something like this is of interest to you, put a responsible friend or family member in charge of your bouquet post-ceremony.

Have a Backup Plan for Boutonnieres
If one or both of you will be wearing a boutonniere, be sure to arrange a backup set with your florist. These are fragile by nature, and after pre-event photography, hugging guests, and anything encountered in the wind, you might need a refreshed version at some point. Also, if you've never put on a boutonniere, it's worth having someone around who has; they're trickier to pin on than you might think.

In the workbook, there's a tab called Floral Checklist. Use this as your go-to place for staying organized with your dream look. Here's an example:

WE DO

FLORAL CHECKLIST

WHEN	ITEM	QTY	FOR
Ceremony			
	Ceremony Arch	1	
	Aisle Markers	2	
Cocktail Hour			
	Bar Arrangements	2	
	Cocktail Tables	2	
	Escort Display	1	
Reception			
	Dining Tables	15	
	Bar Arrangements	2	
	Cake Table	1	
Personals			
	Bouquet Main	1	*Amy*
	Boutonniere Main	1	*Paul*
	Bouquets Supporting	3	*Sarah, Jenny, Susan*
	Boutonnieres Supporting	3	*Harry, David, Peter*
	Toss Petals	1	*Bobby*
	Corsages	0	
	Crowns	1	*Joanne*

SET DECORATION & ACTIVATIONS

CANDLES

If you skipped past the flower section, welcome back! As you've determined for yourself, there are all sorts of other design elements that can enhance and personalize your event. And don't tell my florist friends, but some of them make more of an impact than flowers.

While candles were once the only source of light at night, they're now about as ubiquitous to creating ambience and design for a wedding as couples themselves! The only time you might skip these is if you're having a daytime affair outdoors, as they'll feel a little pointless. But for all other elements of your wedding, use candles wherever possible. They're both romantic and dramatic, they make a space feel special by creating a glow, and you can appreciate their flicker on any reflective materials. Just be sure you understand the rules of your venue when it comes to using candles. Some allow you to use them as you please, while others require all candles be enclosed in some type of glass. Some might even have a required distance from the wick to the top of the vessel. I've planned plenty of outdoor weddings with elements too strong for lit candles and some in wooden barns that simply didn't allow them. Thankfully, there are now battery-operated LED candles that look close to the real thing.

Candles are ideal for more than just tables; they can help illuminate stairways and hallways, and they create a romantic effect when lining a ceremony aisle. Just be sure they're not set anywhere where someone might catch their outfit or hair on fire!

If you're not incorporating flowers into your design or are keeping them minimal, you can choose from endless design ideas that fit your style. One JMK couple was obsessed with the era of Studio 54, so we lined twenty dining tables with disco balls of various sizes and candles to reflect off them. The tables were all named after disco legends, so we had vintage records with names such as Gloria Gaynor marking each table. For a highly theatrical couple, we created table runners made from vintage *Playbills* and topped them with candles and cabaret-style lamps. Vintage books can take us to a love story of another era, while birdcages and bowls of fruit can bring garden-party vibes. One JMK bride had a vision of long ombre tables lined with found objects in the color scheme, so we created that using a series of small statues, figurines, and anything else we could find in the shades of coral and sage she wanted. I've also had clients who needed to keep the tables clear in the center so painted human statues with fruit in their mouths could come to life and entertain guests during dinner. Other couples were a no on flowers and other creative concepts, so we instead created a runner effect of only candles. Any idea you have can grow into your entire vision.

JMK TIP

Don't forget about the unexpected spaces. In-house bathrooms, restroom trailers, hallways, and staircases are all parts of the journey your guests may take. Spice or spruce them up!

LINENS

If your venue provides tables in the sizes that suit your vision, they might also include linens for them. Some include white and ivory while anything else you desire will need to be rented, and others open an entire swatch book for you to choose from. One giant piece of advice I have for you is this: If you can, invest in this fabulous opportunity. If you're looking to make a statement with your tables and don't have enough in your budget for all the florals of your dreams, make a statement with linens. They will do a lot of heavy lifting!

For dining tables and interior bar tables, table coverings should always be measured to hit the floor without puddling on all sides of the table. If you're exploring options for renting linens, be sure you're able to touch and feel them; the texture is nearly impossible to capture in a photo on a website. And whether you're using in-house linens or renting them, be sure to inquire about who'll be in charge of pressing or steaming them in on the day of. Some venues will handle this, while others won't bother. After you've invested all the time and money into your set design, you don't want to ruin it with visible creases or wrinkles. And if you're doing anything outdoors that requires linens, think about using sturdier fabrics. If there's any wind, flapping tablecloths can ruin your set and sometimes even knock off what's on top of the tables. For high tables at outdoor bars, you can arrange to have tablecloths tied at the base or rent a spandex-like cloth. Better yet, get a table that's meant to be naked!

Don't forget the napkins. This is another opportunity for personalization. When I first started out, I was told it was forbidden to have anything other than black napkins because most guests are in black dresses or tuxes. Well, forbidden is a word I don't respond to, and if black napkins aren't part of your vibe, I'm here to tell you your wedding will still be a smash. Whatever color you choose, napkins can be a great way to add color contrast to tables. A dark tablecloth layered with a white plate, dark napkin, and lighter menu is a basic formula for creating something interesting for guests to see when they first sit for dinner.

DRAPING

Draping can be both practical and decorative. If your ceremony and reception are in the same space, drapes might be required to conceal the preset dining tables. If you're getting married in a space that was once a religious venue and you don't want that displayed, drapes can hide things like crosses without damaging a building. They can also hide unsightly views, such as where a caterer might need to set up a satellite kitchen, and they can accentuate the height of ceilings, soften an industrial space, and bring bold colors to your set design. To effectively narrow big openings into smaller spaces and focus the eye, draping can create hallways. And if you want to create a really dramatic effect, a kabuki-style drape can be used to hide something before a reveal and then removed in seconds.

TABLETOPS

If your venue does the food in-house, chances are they include the necessities for tabletops, such as glassware, flatware, and china. However, that doesn't mean it necessarily goes with your vision. And if you're having a wedding that requires all of this to be brought in, you'll need to make these selections anyway.

For tabletop rentals, you first need to assess what's needed for the meal service you chose and then play around with setting the table. Play being an intentional word choice! The number of courses served determines the amount of silverware needed, and your beverage offerings dictate the glassware. Some JMK couples prefer the fuller look of each guest having a separate flute, goblet, or glass for champagne, red wine, white wine, and water. Others prefer a less crowded, more streamlined look that simply includes a water glass and one wine glass for either variety of wine.

One word of caution here: These are decisions you should not be making on your own; the person handling your catering should guide you. You might have some options to discuss with them, however. They might prefer to set the tables with everything needed for all three courses, and you might find that it looks too crowded. You can potentially make adjustments, such as not having bread and butter plates and instead asking for bread to be butlered on people's salad plates. Or you can request that the dessert silverware and coffee setups be placed after dessert or on a station rather than at the tables.

Chargers are an element of event rentals you may or may not respond to. Essentially they're the plate under the plate, but food is never served on them. They come in various shapes and all types of materials, including glass, metal, acrylic, and wicker. They do help a table look more fully set when a guest first sees it, but they might not be your thing if you're the "less is more" type.

SET DECORATION & ACTIVATIONS

JMK TIP

If you like the look of chargers but your budget doesn't allow for them, ask your venue or caterer whether you can instead use entrée plates. The standard service for chargers is that they're removed with the appetizer course, and if the kitchen has plenty of entrée plates and enough time to still plate out the main course, they can pull off the trick of replacing chargers. Want both a menu and a charger for the price of one? Have a menu printed in the shape of a charger!

Once you've settled on what's logistically right for your event's set design, it's time for the fun part. There's an array of designs when it comes to everything needed for meal service. You can go completely gold and gilded, lean into *Mad Men* vibes with cut crystal glassware, go über modern and stemless, or mix floral patterns for something more Boho. And yes, you can have black flatware on a white table! You can also use everything your venue has in-house and simply rent one specialty item, such as blue water goblets, to make a colorful splash on your tables. After reviewing with your caterer and making your selections, be sure to update your rental checklist.

ACTIVATIONS

We've covered the basics of what's needed for the set design of your show, from where your guests will sit and what they'll eat on to how they'll appreciate your set. But are you looking for something a little extra for guests to experience? This is where activations come in, some of which are JMK fan favorites.

■ BEVERAGES

I chose to include beverage activations here because I think of them more as a décor and party element even though technically they serve your guests drinks. Pros design the ice and can etch just about anything into it. We've created ice fountains that drip a continuous pour of a certain beverage; one had "Cheers to Love" on it along with built-in shelves for champagne flutes of chilled Veuve Clicquot that anyone could grab as it was constantly dispensing, and another made a steady stream of vodka sodas and at the top read, "Gay Water." We've also designed many a liquor luge, which are ice sculptures that can be designed as anything and have one spot to pour in a beverage and another where guests drink it as shot. You haven't lived until you've taken a shot of tequila from a unicorn's mouth!

■ **FOR-THE-COUPLE**

For-the-couple activations are those that allow you to take a bit of your wedding home with you. Guest books, for instance, are a traditional way for your guests to leave you a message on your special day. Rather than purchasing a plain book, you can create one that utilizes the photos from your engagement shoot, particularly ones you don't otherwise know what to do with. We've also created a Polaroid guest book station for many JMK couples. There's something about the instant gratification and the surprise of these older cameras that's so fun, especially since we all live in the smartphone era. Guests can put their Polaroids in a book along with a personal note to you.

Rather than providing just a book, I also like giving guests a call to action. Sometimes they respond better with direction. We've often created an anniversary-wish table with instructions and supplies for guests to leave notes for the couple to open on their first, tenth, and twenty-fifth anniversaries. After the event, these are sealed, and the couple can look forward to opening them on these milestones.

Since something like this will be a keepsake for the two of you, think about what you really want to keep. We've

SET DECORATION & ACTIVATIONS

set up a station with a big piece of wood for guests to burn their initials into, a giant wine bottle with corks to be signed by each guest, a canvas of a tree for which guests used paint to make leaves with their fingerprints, and a giant leather-bound book with art supplies telling guests to write the next sentence or draw the next illustration in "The Story of the Couple." For one couple, we worked with an incredible paper artist who had a vision for what the finished piece could be. At the wedding, each guest approached the "Lips Station" where they found a piece of paper with their name on it, selected from an assortment of lipstick shades, and chose the right one to make their pucker. After the wedding, the artist made a giant piece featuring the lips of everyone who attended their wedding! What do you think you'll enjoy most after your show comes to a close?

■ PAINTING

Having live painters at your event can create a nice souvenir for you and your guests. Caricature, portrait, or sketch artists can be hired to complete artwork of individuals, couples, or small groups. If you'd like to offer this to your guests, start by finding the style of art you like most. Some can be a bit cartoony, while others can be high fashion. Be sure to check with the artist or company you're hiring about how many they can complete in one night. While not every guest might participate, you don't want anyone turned away either. You also don't want guests having to sit and pose for a long period of time. Most of these artists snap a photo of who they're drawing so they can paint while guests return to the reception, and guests can pick up their artwork at the end of the night.

You can also have someone create a live painting of your wedding. While this will ultimately be a souvenir for you, guests do enjoy watching this process happen throughout the night. The artist is usually in place before the event, sketching the bones of the venue first, then as guests arrive and the event unfolds, the artist creates a painting capturing the whole affair. This might be a still of one component of the night or a composite capturing different vignettes, such as some people watching the ceremony and others on the dance floor. Many times, the artist takes their canvas home after the event and does the finishing work before sending it to you. If you love the way it turned out, you can not only hang it in your home but use a digital reproduction of the image on your thank-you cards!

■ **Photo Booths**

Photo booths have become standard at many events and in many circles, so I don't think I'm breaking any ground here by suggesting them! The vintage kind found at an old boardwalk prints a strip of photos, which can be fun and nostalgic, and as a huge fan of the movie *Beaches*, I love this kind of thing. There are also kiosks set up on stands, usually in front of some type of backdrop, and guests can operate them using a touch screen. A few styles of these have become quite popular, particularly because they have a way of filtering the photos to make everyone look their best. Who doesn't want that? Trends also include providing a table of silly signs and/or props guests can use while taking photos. If you're interested in these, go for it. I've never witnessed a circumstance in which they're unpopular, and they usually have the capabilities to capture still photos in addition to GIFs, boomerangs, and reels.

In recent years, 360-degree photo booths have become the next big thing. With these devices, a camera fully rotates around the person taking a photo, speeding up and slowing down strategically. Once finished, it creates a little video that goes beyond anyone's selfie capabilities. There's also the roaming photo booth, a device operated by someone who'll be traveling with the crowd throughout the event.

SET DECORATION & ACTIVATIONS

This prevents guests from having to line up for a booth or potentially miss it all together. Then there's photo styling, which means having a dedicated person to not only take the photos but direct your guests on poses. We often refer to this as the "*Vanity Fair* booth." I've found that guests love this because they appreciate and benefit from someone telling them to lower their chin or remove from their pocket the hand that's causing a bulge.

With any of these options, you'll likely have a choice between on-site printing, digital receipt, or both. While taking home a newly printed picture is nice, digital photos can be shared by your guests right away, and there's usually an option for them to order a print if they really love one. If you're printing on-site, you can have two copies of each photo made, and guests can take one and leave the other with a note in a book for you.

In addition to how they're distributed, be sure to review the borders and any text or graphic that gets laid on top. It can be as simple as your names and the date or a logo, or it can be something altogether silly.

■ **STYLING**

For many, attending a wedding is like being part of a fantasy. And if that's what you want for your guests, you need to set them up for success! Styling activations can be in the form of a self-service station, such as a table where all the supplies are provided for making flower crowns or friendship bracelets, or they can have attendants, such as henna or glitter stations. Yes, we've set up makeup artists stocked with glitter, lashes, and jewels to give any guest's face a little something extra.

And finally, there's the wig bar. For countless JMK clients, both gay and straight, it's not uncommon for a bunch of wigs to come out that let people express themselves more fully or as alter egos. After these requests kept growing, we elevated this into a full styling station with multiple types and colors of wigs displayed on wig heads, plus sunglasses, costume jewelry, and of course mirrors and brushes so guests can perfect their transformation. They've been a huge hit with guests of all demographics!

Yes, it's that time again. Visit the workbook and scroll to the tab Purchase List. Here's where you can be sure everything you won't be renting is accounted for. Take a look at this example:

SET DECORATION & ACTIVATIONS

WHEN	ITEM	QTY	LINK	ORDERED
Ceremony				
	Pillar Candles	12		☐
	Glass Cylinders	12		☐
	Program Basket	1		☐
Cocktail Hour				
	Card Box	1		☐
	Fun Fact Napkins	250		☐
	Dog Cocktail Stirrers	100		☐
Reception				
	Wig Heads	12		☐
	Wigs	36		☐
	Sunglasses	75		☐
	Glow Sticks	100		☐

Do you feel inspired to decorate your set and maybe add some immersive experiences for your guests, or do you feel like lip stations and wigs are a hard pass? Remember: Décor and activations are for your guests. Now it's time to talk about the two of you! I'll see you in the next chapter to discuss what the VIPs will be wearing.

Chapter 11

COSTUME DESIGN

Selecting what you wear to your wedding is one of the most personal parts of this process. If you don't show up to your wedding feeling your best, you likely won't enjoy all the hard work you put into planning it. Perhaps more than anything else, your wedding fashion is an element where you can really express your authentic self, feel the fantasy of your day, and push the boundaries if you choose to do so. Remember: You're dressing for yourself, your partner, and all the photos and videos that will be captured and live on forever. So no pressure!

When clients hire me as a full-service wedding planner, they ask whether there's anything my services don't cover. My response is always the same: "We handle everything other than wardrobe, jewelry, and your honeymoon. But we do have recommendations for experts in those fields and can happily pair you with a stylist and travel agent." While we remind couples about important tasks in their calendars, such as initial shopping and final fittings, wedding attire is personal.

If you're completely lost on where to look and what to look for, this is a job for a best friend, sibling, parent, or professional. And in this inclusive book, I'm certainly not one to say jackets are only for grooms and trains are only for brides. I've seen wedding fashion expressed across the spectrum. Any couple who chooses to wear something authentic and executes it in a way that harmonizes fit, style, and proportion looks nothing less than runway ready.

STYLE

Some of you may have dreamed about what you'd wear to your wedding since you were very young and have an excellent idea of what you're looking for. Others just know their style. I've had grooms marry in matching chinos, polos, and harnesses, and I've had brides in just about every color other than white or ivory to better suit their style.

Many JMK couples need to take some time to discover their style. The first step is identifying some notion of what you want to find. Your vision for the event should help inform this. If you're getting married barefoot on a beach, chances are a long beaded train isn't for you. And if you've asked your guests to show up in their Met Gala best, you won't be saying vows in shorts and flip flops. You'll also need to consider what time of year the wedding will be, what the weather will be like, and whether your wedding will have any outdoor components. If you'll already be drenched in sweat from pre-ceremony photos, you won't feel your best when walking down the aisle. Start browsing the internet and social media with searches that speak to you, such as "cutting-edge fashion-forward bride," "timeless dapper black-tie groom," or "gender nonconforming nonbinary marrying person." Unless one or both of you are the type with no affinity for fashion, this should be one of the most fun assignments. And if you're one of them, don't overcomplicate this. Just find something you feel comfortable in.

For my LGBTQ+ couples, you might have a few more decisions than a straight couple. If you don't instinctively know, ask yourselves these questions:

COSTUME DESIGN

- Do we want to coordinate?
- Do we want to match head to toe?
- Do we want to contrast?
- Do we even care about this?

Your wedding fashion is a chance to let your personalities shine, celebrate both the differences and the similarities between the two of you, and further the overall design of your event. Remember: You are the stars of the night, so don't be afraid to go a bit bolder than your normal look. You can say so much through color, texture, and fit. Be wary of options that resemble costumes unless that's a deliberate choice. And if you selected colors for your wedding, don't feel you have to wear them; a beautiful color like turquoise usually works better for a tablecloth than a tuxedo.

If you're having trouble deciding what look to go for, my suggestion is to opt for something *you* consider classic. You'll have your wedding photos forever, and you want to look back and say, "We looked great!" not "What the hell were we thinking?!" When searching for something classic, it doesn't necessarily need to be from this year's collection. A design from a different season will cost less, and nobody other than you and Tan France will know the difference. Don't feel like you have to spend the money on couture to feel like a model. Sadly, this is one place where there's a bit of gender disparity. Most people who purchase a bridal gown find that they never have an opportunity to wear it again, but a new suit, tux romper, or pantsuit can be rocked multiple times.

Start looking early enough so you can enjoy the process of finding your special outfit rather than being stressed and making anxiety-driven purchases. As you browse, you'll discover you might be able to wear something off the rack, something that requires tailoring, or something that's totally custom. That last option tends to be the most expensive, but who can put a price tag on something truly made only for you?

For those of you looking for a dress or gown, the next section is for you; you'll feel less overwhelmed if you identify some of your preferences before you go shopping! If gowns and dresses aren't for you, feel free to skip ahead to accessories.

SILHOUETTES & NECKLINES

Modern-day bridal fashion is quite exciting and constantly offering new concepts, but there are some tried and true basics. Besides the silhouette, the neckline of a dress can influence how you wear your hair, what jewelry you accessorize with, and which undergarments you'll need based on how modest or busty you've chosen to go. You'll notice some comments about what's typically suggested to be the most flattering for different body types, but I want to stress that you are welcome to defy convention. What's most important is what *you* think of how it looks and how *you* feel while wearing it.

- **SILHOUETTES**
  - The *A-line* silhouette is named for the shape made from something that's fitted through the waist and flared out below. This shape tends to be flattering to any body type and is great for disguising the hips if you think they're a problem area.
  - *Ball gown* sounds like an object from a fairy tale, and this silhouette is meant to look like one. Gowns with this silhouette are fitted on the top and flare below the waist with incredible volume. This silhouette can be distracting if you feel you're pear-shaped.
  - Dresses with *empire* silhouettes are fitted at the very top, but the waistline is drawn underneath the bust rather than at the natural waist. This shape is flattering on most body types and is bump-friendly should you be expecting.
  - A *mermaid* silhouette hugs the torso and shows off the figure down to the knees where it flares out. This can be ideal if you're narrower at the bottom or simply want to show off what you've got on top.

COSTUME DESIGN

A-line

Ball gown

Empire

Mermaid

SILHOUETTES

WE DO

Sheath

Short

Trumpet

SILHOUETTES

- A *sheath* silhouette lies close to the body with a straight-cut fit and zero waist seam. It can be less forgiving if you have areas you'd rather hide.
- Garments with a *short* silhouette are technically considered dresses, not gowns, but if you don't want something that hits the ground you could opt for a short silhouette in tea length (above the ankle), midi (between knee and ankle), or mini (above the knee).
- A *trumpet* silhouette hugs the torso and shows off everything until mid-thigh where it flares out and makes the shape of the instrument it's named for. Similar to the mermaid, this brings attention to what you have on top.

■ Necklines

- An *asymmetrical* or one-shoulder neckline has a strap only on one side.
- *Bateau* is a high neckline that grazes the collarbone.
- *Halter* is a neckline with straps that come together in the back, showing off the shoulders in the front.
- A *high* neckline sits close to the chin and provides the most coverage.
- The *jewel* neckline is sometimes referred to as the "T-shirt neckline" because it's rounded at the collarbones.
- With an *off-the-shoulder* neckline, fabric is draped around the upper arms, leaving the shoulders and collarbones to shine.
- A *plunging* neckline is a dramatic cut and a bold way to elongate your torso and bring attention to your bust.
- *Scoop* or *U-neck* shapes are circular and provide additional support.
- As its name suggests, a *square* neckline has right angles.

WE DO

NECKLINES

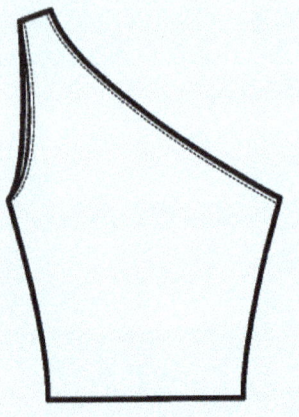
Asymmetrical

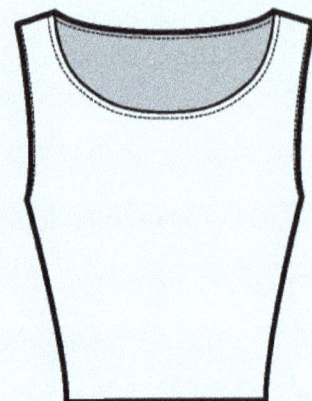
Bateau

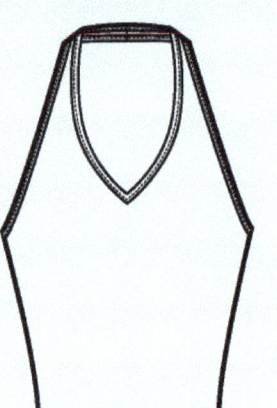
Halter

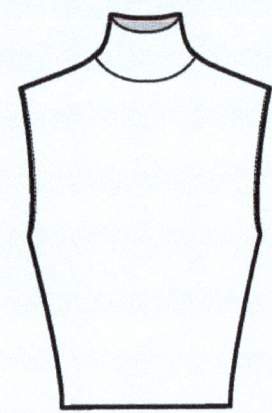
High

Jewel

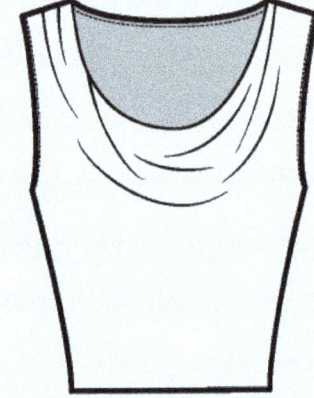
Off-the-shoulder

250

COSTUME DESIGN

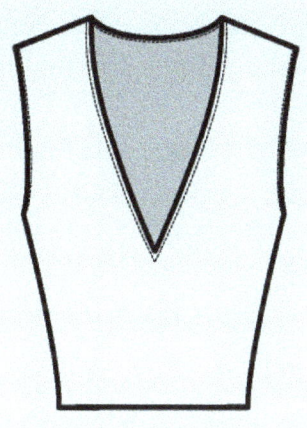
Plunging

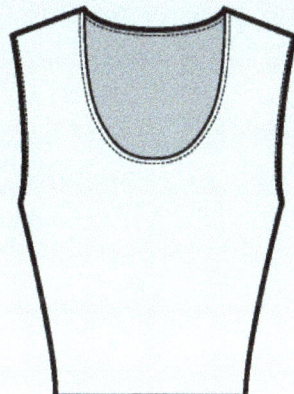
Scoop or U-neck

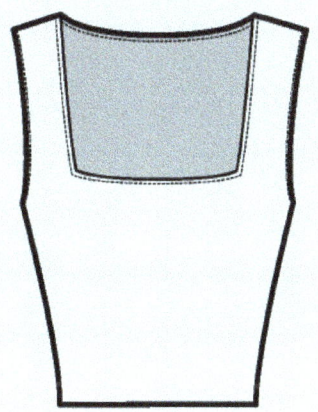
Square

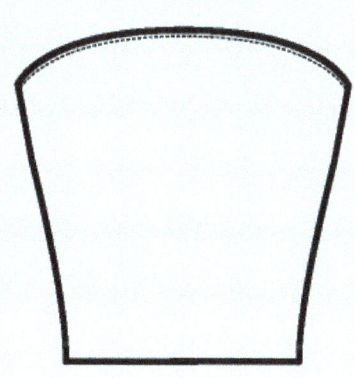
Strapless

Sweetheart

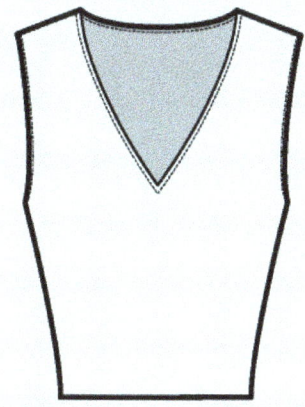
V-neck

NECKLINES

- A *strapless* neckline usually goes straight across the breasts and leaves everything above exposed.
- A *sweetheart* neckline resembles the top half of a heart and accentuates the bust, and it's usually strapless.
- A *V-neck* elongates the torso and usually has straps.

FABRICS, COLORS & FINISHES

Now that you have the ABCs of shapes, it's time to think about what they're made of. Ideally, the staff where you're shopping will be able to weigh in on the pros and cons of what has gone into their dresses. Most commonly they're made from batiste, brocade, charmeuse, chiffon, crepe, damask, faille, illusion lace, organza, satin, shantung, silk, taffeta, tulle, or velvet, and the most common colors are white, ivory, and champagne. Fabrics can also be further enhanced by beads, lace, embroidery, and appliques. It's a lot to consider, which is one of many reasons for multiple seasons of TV shows documenting the process of finding a wedding dress. I'm simply trying to whet your palette of knowledge here, so if you feel a red sequined pantsuit is your wedding look, I'm in full support!

TRAINS

For some, the train is their favorite part of a dress, while others don't want one at all. A train is meant to drag on the ground, so it's not ideal for outdoor weddings and/or outdoor pre-wedding photos. If you'll be walking down an indoor aisle, you won't want your train covered in mud or anything else it can pick up during outdoor portraits. You'll need to be mindful of this and whether the train is fully detachable from your dress. If it isn't, it will need to be bustled, so be sure to dedicate a responsible person to bustling you at the wedding. Also make sure to practice this in advance! A dress not cooperating is a surefire way to get a wedding completely off schedule.

COSTUME DESIGN

JMK TIP

At your fitting, get a video of how the dress is bustled. If your dedicated bustler can't be at the fitting, they can watch it as a guide. And if for any reason they aren't capable of fulfilling the duty at the wedding (maybe they took one too many trips to the open bar), the video will save time for the understudy.

VEILS

There are various old customs preventing a groom from changing his mind when he sees the bride for the first time, protecting him from evil forces, and confirming he's marrying who he intends, and wearing a veil is one of them. While there's a decent chance that none of those reasons speak to you, many prefer a veil simply because it looks nice with a dress. If you're one of them, be sure to look for a veil that complements your overall look and consider how it attaches. Many JMK couples take pre-event photos without the veil and add it right before the ceremony, but that's not the time for scrambling to see how it stays attached!

If you're looking to add sentimental value, a veil can be your something borrowed. If not, there's a booming industry complete with magazines, stores, and designers that specialize in bridal fashion. Whether you're looking to fully immerse yourself in this world or chart a path of least resistance, do not procrastinate on this! Many JMK brides were shocked to learn that securing a dress and all the fittings it requires may take eight to twelve months. Do not underestimate the amount of time fittings will take, and do not be afraid to ask for something that makes it a bit more perfect for you. If you find something sleeveless you love but would rather have your arms covered for the ceremony, see whether it can be offered with removable sleeves.

SUITS & TUXES

For those of you looking for a suit or tux, this is the section for you. A lot of what I lay out here relates to what's considered "formal wear," but it's good to understand the basics, so just make these your own.

■ CLASSIC OPTIONS
1. *Black tie*, or tuxedo styles, can range in design and are considered the standard for a formal occasion.
2. *White tie* is a step above black tie. It's for something super formal and includes a tailcoat and a white tie.
3. A *suit* is one step down in terms of formality, but it can be appropriate for dressy occasions or when wanting to be more informal, such as when worn with an open collar and no tie.

While each of these options come in many colors, it's probably no surprise that black is what's most common. If you're looking for something a little different without going too bold, then navy or gray can be nice options. I've also had grooms wear all white, and personally I'm the proud owner of suits and tuxedos in just about every color and many bold patterns.

■ JACKETS
Whichever palette you decide on, the jacket is where the majority of the personality is. There are four main jacket styles and fits:

1. A *single-breasted cut* is classic and suited to most body types. It's elongating and can be worn closed (top button only) or open.
2. A *double-breasted cut* can add a bit of bulk, so it doesn't work on as many body types and is worn only closed.

COSTUME DESIGN

Black tie

White tie

Suit

WE DO

JACKETS

Single-breasted cut

Double-breasted cut

Stroller

Tailcoat

3. A *stroller* can technically be single or double breasted, the key difference being it lacks the satin accents of a tuxedo jacket.
4. A *tailcoat* can have two options that define you as "wearing tails." A dress coat is the most formal, has a square cutaway front, and is worn only in the evening. A morning coat, which is considered more suitable for a formal daytime affair, is cut away at the front in a gradual taper.

Pay close attention to the cut and fit of the jacket. If the vent in the back is pulling open, it's too tight. The "button stance," which can be high or low, is a tailoring term for where the buttons are placed on a jacket. A lower stance is elongating and better suited for most body types, while a high stance usually looks better on those who are tall and slim. Jackets should always hug the shoulders perfectly rather than too much or not enough, and the sleeves of the jacket should be long enough or hemmed to the wrist, which allows about half an inch of the shirt to show.

■ Lapels

The lapel can sometimes be the star of a jacket, but you'll want to pay attention to the vents and fabric it's made of.

1. A *notch* is average in size and usually cut out between the collar and lapel.
2. A *peak* is when the top of the lapel is peaked up and out, and it's larger so it can bring some drama to the look.
3. A *shawl* is when there's no break between the collar and lapel, which can give a bit of a vintage look with its rounded line.

■ Pants

Most well-designed suits or tuxes have a matching or corresponding set of pants, and the fit is extremely important.

WE DO

LAPELS

Notch

Peak

Shawl

You don't want anything unnecessarily baggy or oversized unless that's an intentional fashion statement. You also want the pants to button easily without you having to suck it all in the entire night. Trust me, you won't last! If you're wearing tuxedo pants with a side stripe, it's usually preferable for the hem to brush the top of the shoe. With stripeless pants, the hem should break around the laces, covering about a third of it. But again, these are classic guidelines that were once considered a must. I've had grooms hem their pants shorter and pair them with dress shoes without socks and brides wear tuxedo jackets with an intentional sexy bra poking through.

■ Shirts

Once you have the outer pieces in place, you'll need to find the right shirt. If you're wearing a suit, you can play around a bit with the collar. For a tuxedo with a bowtie, you'll want a shirt with either a winged, turndown, spread, or pointed collar and sleeves that have either barrel or French cuffs.

Whether you're someone looking for a dress, gown, suit, tux, or onesie, you'll be able to find some of these items for rent. While some companies have come a long way in what they offer in rentals, their clothing rarely looks made-to-measure.

ACCESSORIES

Once you've determined the main element or elements of your wedding look, it's time to accessorize. You might have already chosen something bold with your main pieces, but sometimes it's these smaller details that not only complete the look but really let your personality shine through.

■ Cufflinks & Studs

There's no better way to personalize your look than with a little jewelry, which is considered required with a French cuff shirt. This might be one of the few opportunities for you to wear something with sentimental value that has been passed down or a time to make a really fun statement.

■ Cummerbunds & Vests

It was once considered standard to wear either a cummerbund or a vest with a tuxedo, and they usually matched the tie and covered the waist of the pants. However, fashion has evolved, and now you can choose one, the other, or neither. Keep in mind that cummerbunds draw attention to the waist, so if you're looking to hide that area, a vest is better for your body type. If you're wearing a bow tie, you can wear either a cummerbund or a vest, but a necktie should be paired only with a vest. And yes, you can go without either and still pull off a wonderfully formal look in a tuxedo.

■ Jewelry

Whether you're a bride, a groom, or a different title all together, consider what other jewelry besides what you might be exchanging during the ceremony will complete your look. This can include earrings, necklaces, bracelets, watches, hair jewels, tiaras, broaches, boutonnieres, and tie pins. This can also be a wonderful place to incorporate an heirloom. Maybe you have jeweled panties, as it's a special night. I'll get to undergarments in a bit!

■ Kerchief or Pocket Square

Having a kerchief or a pocket square in your jacket pocket is an excellent fashion detail. A stiff, white triangle looks very classy on a black tuxedo, while bright colors or patterns make a fun statement on a suit. There are several different folds you can do for either. If you're going to wear

COSTUME DESIGN

a boutonniere, just make sure you consider the kerchief as well because they should complement each other, not clash.

- **SHOES**

Unless you're getting married barefoot on the beach, shoes are an essential accessory. Some people, of any gender, easily do heels. I've done plenty of weddings for people who lasted from pre-event photos to the last dance wearing four-inch Louboutins, but I've done more weddings for people who thought they could or wanted to do that but could barely walk before they got to the aisle. You must have "shoe truth" with yourself. What can you realistically stand, walk, and dance in?

If your dream is to take your getting-ready portraits and ceremony shots in high heels but you can't imagine wearing them throughout the event, it's perfectly acceptable to change footwear, just be certain to bring to your final fitting all shoes you'll be wearing. Practice walking in the shoes at home (inside so you don't risk getting them scuffed), and make sure all versions work with your look. As long as those bedazzled Converse work when the dress is bustled, you'll be fine. And trust me, the expression "foot fashion can be painful" isn't limited to heels. I've seen so many grooms buy a pair of designer dress shoes without spending any advance time in them, only to complain at the wedding as though they'd been forced into stilettos.

Also consider an option for potential rain. One JMK bride got married during a monsoon, and she told me that one of the best decisions she made was shopping for an inexpensive pair of shoes to throw on when she went outside to take photos. Once back inside, she returned to her nicer pair for the rest of the night.

- **SOCKS**

You wouldn't forget to put socks on with your dress shoes, but you might forget to find a special pair before the big day.

Socks are a playful opportunity for a reveal when you sit or during some dancing, and they're a fun way to flash a bold color or pattern.

■ SUSPENDERS & BELTS

Tuxedo pants were originally made without belt loops, and men were expected to use suspenders to keep their pants up. Now many people wear them simply for the look rather than needing them to keep their pants in place. Many tuxedos are also now designed with belt loops, and if you have them you should wear a belt. If you're on the shorter side, a belt can draw attention to a horizontal break in your body and a pair of suspenders can elongate you. Just be sure your suspenders or belt complement or match the color of your shoes.

■ TIE OR BOW TIE

For a suit or tux, you'll have to consider some additional accessories, and this can be another place where you can really let your personality shine. There's definitely no right or wrong here, and both regular ties and bow ties work in modern fashion for all levels of formality. With either option, the fabric should complement the jacket's lapel. For a bow tie, there's nothing like a classic one (versus a clip-on) unless it's made of a fabric like velvet or material for which that's the only possibility, such as feathers, jewels, or wood. If you're going with a classic bow tie and aren't adept at tying one, be sure to practice before the big day. It's a technique not easily achieved on the first attempt.

■ UNDERGARMENTS

Undergarments should not be undervalued for any gender or gender expression. They're important for everyone. Whether you want Spanx to smooth out your figure, a bra to lift or minimize your bust, an undershirt to prevent sweating, or a G-string as your something blue, purchase them in advance and try them on along with your main garments to ensure you have everything you need. And don't forget to bring them to your fittings!

I know this is a lot to remember as you work toward assembling all the pieces that will make you shine and feel your best. That's why you'll find the Shopping and Pack List Worksheet in our workbook. As you identify what's required for your final look, be sure to add every single element so you don't forget to buy them or pack them for the big event afterward. I've seen many regretful couples who simply "forgot their special cufflinks," and I want to set you up for success as much as possible. Here's an example for when you're just getting started:

WE DO

MUTUAL	PURCHASED	PACKED	SPOUSE 1	PURCHASED	PACKED
Marriage License	☐	☐	Dress	☐	☐
Rings	☐	☐	Shoes	☐	☐
Invitation Suite For Photos	☐	☐	Veil	☐	☐
	☐	☐	Jewelry	☐	☐
	☐	☐	Undergarments	☐	☐
	☐	☐	Wedding Party Gifts	☐	☐
	☐	☐	Getting Ready Outfit	☐	☐
	☐	☐		☐	☐
	☐	☐		☐	☐
	☐	☐		☐	☐
	☐	☐		☐	☐
	☐	☐		☐	☐
	☐	☐		☐	☐
	☐	☐		☐	☐
	☐	☐		☐	☐

SHOPPING & PACK LIST

COSTUME DESIGN

SPOUSE 2	PUR-CHASED	PACKED	PACK OUT ITEMS	
Suit	☐	☐	Escort Cards	☐
Shoes	☐	☐	Cocktail Napkins	☐
Shirt	☐	☐	Extra Programs	☐
Tie	☐	☐	Gifts/Cards	☐
Cufflinks	☐	☐	Top Tier of Cake	☐
Belt	☐	☐		☐
Socks	☐	☐		☐
Wedding Party Gifts	☐	☐		☐
	☐	☐		☐
	☐	☐		☐
	☐	☐		☐
	☐	☐		☐
	☐	☐		☐
	☐	☐		☐
	☐	☐		☐

SHOPPING & PACK LIST

GROUP LOOKS

Regardless of what you're calling them, if you're having a wedding party of any kind, it's important to give them direction and advance notice. Traditional weddings usually involve a bride picking out the dress she wants her bridesmaids to wear in addition to some coordinating look for all the groomsmen. For many nontraditional couples, the concept of a group look doesn't fit, but it should still be considered. Choose what feels right for you. You can go the more expected route and ask everyone to match, or you can unify a group by giving them a color scheme to stick with or a fashion motif to follow, such as black suits and long black dresses. You could ask everyone to wear khaki pants and a shirt of one color, or you could tell everyone to wear animal prints. You could also choose to have all those in a suit wear the same one, while one or both of you stand out by having a different vest or tie. Just realize something like this takes more coordination in making everyone purchase (or rent) the matching looks. It's also important to give fashion guidelines to those who aren't technically in your party but are people of honor, such as parents, even if it's just a color scheme.

In addition, you must think about everyone getting ready. This is one of those elements of wedding planning that can range from incredibly simple to annoyingly complex. First of all, you must decide what both of you need to get ready on the day of, which may or may not be the same. Traditionally, brides get ready with all the other females involved and avoid seeing the groom until the first look. For the record, I've had plenty of straight clients who that didn't speak to, so they opted to get ready together. With LGBTQ+ couples, I've seen it done several ways, from those who choose to be completely separate during this time and avoid seeing one another to those who share in the experience. Really think about how you want to spend the "getting ready" portion of your wedding day.

With that decided, it's time to book the required professionals. Hair and makeup artists aren't limited by gender, and we often book them to assist everyone. Most JMK brides have hair and makeup

COSTUME DESIGN

trials in advance of the wedding, which allows them to explore the styles they think might work best with their look. This is called a trial for a reason: If you're not happy with the result, you have time to ask for modification. Most JMK grooms don't have a trial unless they have longer hair that's intricate to style. For grooms wearing makeup, it's usually intended to appear as if they're not wearing any and are just miraculously glowing and a bit smoother. If you look ready to compete in the next season of *Drag Race*, you went too far, unless that was intentional. Regardless of gender, light makeup can hide any tired spots from the exhausting last few weeks of planning and often makes a huge difference in your photos.

If you're choosing to have separate experiences, you must identify how many people will be getting ready and in how many locations. Discuss with the artists the specifics of how many people will be getting full hair and makeup versus how many will need light styling. From there you can work with them to create a realistic schedule that keeps everyone on time.

Besides the beautification that can happen on the day of, there are some other common practices you might want to build into your calendar in advance, such as those that are forthcoming. These may not speak to you at all, but if they do, be sure to leave the appropriate amount of time for them.

LET'S GET PHYSICAL

You've probably heard the term "wedding diet" more than once, as it's quite common for this special day to motivate someone more than ever before. If you're one of those incredibly lucky people who are always photo-shoot-ready, then not only do most of us envy you, but you can keep up your routine and move on. For the rest, you might want to find some extra determination to hit the gym, try a new fitness craze, or simply up your normal routine. Even if you don't need to lose weight, exercise increases your energy levels and is a great outlet for some of the stress you'll experience from planning a wedding.

Diet goes hand in hand with exercise. Aside from the bonus of shedding a few extra pounds the camera might add, you'll want to feel your healthiest for such an important occasion. Whether it's for a week, a month, or a year, cutting out vices and junk food can do wonders for clearing your skin and mind. Plus, when you finally make it to your wedding, indulging will never taste better. There are many well-known supplements now that help you curb your appetite and shed weight, and for some of you your wedding might be the reason to finally dabble. Just be weary of trying anything new too close to the big day in case you have any negative side effects.

JMK TIPS

Don't Change Too Much

Don't wither away or get too bulky, especially since it affects the way your fabulous fashion fits. There's a balance between looking your best and complete transformation, so be sure not to change too drastically after your fittings.

Don't Overdo It

If your pre-wedding regimen is drastically different from your regular habits, be careful about overdoing it when you return to the land of your old self. If you seriously detox, your favorite cocktail will hit you stronger and the rich food might be harder to digest. If you want to do an official cleanse, plan it to conclude with enough time to transition back to your preferred eating and drinking habits.

I FEEL PRETTY

In addition to getting your body in the best shape possible for your wedding, you'll want to think about putting some other services into your calendar. If you already enjoy being pampered, much of this will be familiar. If you're new to this, what better reason than your own wedding to indulge?

■ Botox

For many of you, getting Botox might be as common as going to the grocery store. For others, this might be your first time getting injections that freeze parts of your face and eliminate some wrinkles and lines. This magic eraser is a great tool, but be sure you can still show some emotion on your wedding day.

■ Facial

If you've never experienced pampering to the point of having your skin exfoliated and hydrated, I highly recommend it. It's a great way to not only relax but get your skin more photo ready. You can also look into more extreme procedures such as chemical peels, but do not do one the morning of or the day before, and be sure to consult with your practitioner about the recommended recovery time.

■ Facial Hair

My advice on facial hair really applies to everyday life, not just to your wedding day. There's no reason to have a unibrow or overgrown nose hair. If you're prone to either, get rid of them before your photos. But do not decide to start tweezing your own eyebrows on your wedding day! With the excitement and stress you'll likely be feeling, it would be easy to accidentally overdo it, and there's no turning back! If you've waited until the last minute, have a professional or friend take care of this so that it's done within reason.

■ Haircut

Unless you're intending to rock a freshly shaved head, be sure to get a new haircut with enough time for it to grow in slightly. If you plan to add extensions, I recommend doing this with enough time to grow accustomed to the extra length, especially if this will be your first foray with them. Do not use your wedding as an opportunity to try out that crazy haircut you've been scared to try. Yes, I encourage everyone to be bold, but this could be something you end up regretting when you look at your photos.

■ MANICURE & PEDICURE

While I know some of you enjoy getting a mani-pedi as much as you enjoy grabbing an iced latte at Starbucks, others have never been buffed. Your wedding is a time when people and cameras will look at your hands, so they should look their best. Some may feel this doesn't apply to feet, but if you're already going to the salon, treat yourself. It feels fantastic! And if you're wearing open-toed shoes, it's a must! If you're a nail biter, find a way to quit this habit a few weeks before. Manicurists aren't miracle workers!

■ MASSAGE

I personally can't think of a better way to relax than having a professional massage, especially leading up to your special day. If you don't have time for an indulgent spa day, even a fifteen-minute neck and shoulder massage during which you disconnect from emails and spreadsheets can make a world of difference in how you feel. Book this in advance so you can enjoy it at a time that's convenient for you; it defeats the purpose if you're stressed the whole time! After all, isn't the whole reason for planning a wedding to have a happy ending?

■ PROFESSIONAL SHAVE

For those of you with facial hair, a professional shave is another wonderful indulgence I highly recommend. If you're not going to spring for it, at least use a new blade on your wedding day. If you're on the hairier side and prone to a five o'clock shadow, pack a razor and shaving cream to take with you to the wedding so you can do a quick touch-up after the ceremony. If you have sensitive skin, test out a professional shave in advance. If your skin doesn't react well, you know to skip this on the day of.

■ SWEAT CONTROL

If you're one of those people who sweat uncontrollably or unexplainably (a condition known as hyperhidrosis), use your wedding as an opportunity to do something about it. Sweating is heightened during times of stress, and if you look down and see pit stains during your vows, it's only going to stress you more. Try some of the over-the-counter options first. If they don't work, see a dermatologist. If no options are right for you and you're concerned, wear a black or dark-colored shirt as part of your attire. It won't stop the sweat, but it will make the stains less noticeable.

■ TEETH

You'll be smiling in many photos, and if you're even a little self-conscious about your teeth's shade of white, now is the time to get them as pearly as possible. If you apply any kind of do-it-yourself treatment, be sure to do so evenly.

■ TANNING

There's nothing like having a healthy glow in photos. We all have different skin tones, and I know this section doesn't apply to everyone, such as those fair types who avoid the sun or those with naturally dark complexions. But for many of us, having just a little extra color makes a difference. However, I emphasize the word *little*. If you have time to take in some sun in small doses in the weeks before your wedding, then go for it. But if you're pressed for time, have a spray tan done a few days before. You can go into a booth that you operate, or even better, spring to have a professional spray you. With real sun or spray tans, be sure to keep your skin color looking natural. A sunburned or orange couple is not the look you want!

Remember: All of this is food for thought. You should feel comfortable with anything you're going to wear and any treatment you're going to get. It's your day, and if it's done your way, nothing will stop you from feeling like a wedding star.

Don't forget to use the workbook as your number one tool for organization. Once you get your fitting schedule, add the specific dates to your master calendar. And once you have everything secured that you'll need, be sure the pack list is filled out in entirety. Having this to review when you are actually packing will guarantee nothing is forgotten!

With your fashion and beauty plan in place, do you feel ready to move on to the final steps of planning? I'll see you before opening night!

Chapter 12

OPENING NIGHT

We've now gone through every step necessary to write, budget for, book, direct, cast, advertise, document, compose, nourish, design, decorate, dress, and rehearse your show. Now, at long last, it's time to prepare for opening night. As the date draws closer, you'll need to deal with some final logistics to avoid unnecessary stress.

As a planner, I work diligently to understand the nuances and needs of every couple and their guests, and if you've made it to this point and are still the two people mainly in charge, you must do the same for you and your guests. The goal, although not always realistically achieved, is to avoid your guests trying to message you on the weekend because they're confused about where to go or where to be. Even when we triple check that every scenario is accounted for and distribute all this information, some people still choose not to read it, but at least you can feel you did your part.

FINAL NUMBERS & SEATING

A few weeks before your event is when your RSVPs are due, but trust me, you will still have maybes or people you have to chase. Don't be afraid to reach out to people you haven't heard from. If they haven't responded by the due date, they're the ones at fault. Be understanding and leave room for honest mistakes, but try to cross every T and dot every I.

Once you have your final RSVP count, or at least one pretty close to it, you'll need to work on your seating plan if you're having one. This is a notoriously stressful task, so I encourage you to start it early and accept that this is never a perfect science. Most of you will find grouping people together for tables is easy at first, then you'll reach the last 10 percent of your list and find that it doesn't make sense to seat those guests with one another. Remember: This is *your* wedding. If you have to put some people who don't know each other together at a table, that's okay. Who knows, you might even turn out to be a matchmaker. The most important thing is to avoid inadvertently provoking unnecessary conflicts by seating family or exes who don't get along with one another. If you have many different generations of people in attendance, it's a good rule of thumb to try placing the older people where it might be a bit quieter rather than on top of the music. But again, if this becomes impossible, don't lose too much sleep. It's assigned seating at a wedding, not an all-day conference.

Once you've finalized seating, look over the proofs of how this is being communicated to guests, whether it's escort cards, a seating chart, or something more creative. It's never a bad idea to have a few blanks for last-minute changes, but if a request can't be accommodated, it's perfectly acceptable to verbally communicate that to a guest. You'll also have to submit a final head count to your caterer or venue, and at that point you can no longer reduce, even if you have a cancelation. This does happen often because people get sick or flights get canceled.

OPENING NIGHT

JMK TIP

If you can get away with it, it doesn't hurt to under-confirm by a few. Venues and caterers should be able to accommodate you if you end up having 100 percent attendance. You'll likely still be billed, but this way you might avoid paying for guests who don't show up.

ACCOMMODATIONS & WELCOME BAGS

If you've reserved a block of rooms at a hotel, be sure to reach out for a rooming list as soon as the block cutoff date passes. If any guests waited until the last minute and are still in need of booking, you can check whether the hotel has an option of adding rooms or extending the cutoff date. As the week of the event approaches, ask for the final rooming list. If you know of out-of-town guests who'll be attending but they're not on the list, verify to make sure they either booked outside the block (this happens often if guests have a point system with a hotel brand) or have made other arrangements all together.

Welcome bags or arrival gifts are a nice touch for out-of-town guests. They don't have to be elaborate, but this gesture shows how much you appreciate them for traveling. You can compose a personal welcome letter, which can be short and sweet, or create a thorough brochure of the vacation your guests will experience. Be sure to include a thank you and a rundown of the weekend's festivities, and list times when they're supposed to be at specific places, such as when the shuttle will depart from the hotel or where the farewell brunch will be. Also give some suggestions for local activities, restaurants, and tourist attractions they can enjoy during their downtime.

This can also be a fun opportunity to personalize and bring another aspect of yourselves to experience that doesn't fit in elsewhere, such as treats from your hometown. We've organized welcome bags that range from a simple snack, a bottle of water, and a note to those as elaborate as what you might find at a royal wedding! Here's a list of suggestions to brainstorm with:

- The actual bags, which could be gift bags, customized totes, decorative boxes, or other creative packaging
- A welcome letter with the schedule and other points of interest for the weekend
- Something to drink, either a bottle of water or something more specific that fits the overall vision of your wedding
- A snack, which could be something local, something specific to you as a couple, or your favorite snack
- Anything else that you think your guests might need for the weekend, such as over-the-counter headache relief, a little hangover cure, matches, hair ties . . . the possibilities are endless

Remember: Welcome bags are typically designed as one per couple or one per room, not one per guest. Be sure to communicate these parameters with your hotel.

JMK TIP

If your guests are staying at multiple places, getting welcome bags to each location can be challenging. It's perfectly acceptable to have them displayed at a welcome party. And if assembling them isn't your thing, you can set up a "make your own gift bag" station at the event and let guests take what they want!

OPENING NIGHT

TRANSPORTATION

When organizing transportation, you need to consider both you and your guests. Would the two of you like to really make a splash by arriving and/or departing in a limo, on horses, in a vintage car, on jet skis, on bicycles for two, or in a hot air balloon? Whether you're interested in something showy or practical, you'll need to confirm all the details in advance so that you and your guests arrive on time. I recommend not being glued to your phone on the wedding day, so assign someone as the point of contact for transportation who can liaise with a driver or a captain, whether it's someone in your wedding party or your photographer.

If you and your wedding party will all be getting ready off-site, traveling to the venue together can be part of the experience. It also can help ensure the day stays on schedule. If you're booking a vehicle, be sure to consider the size of the group, but if you're all staying where the wedding is taking place, you don't have to worry about this.

What about your guests? If you have a lot of out-of-towners and they aren't staying at the wedding venue, providing transportation for them not only is a lovely and practical gesture but ensures they'll arrive on time and won't drive home drunk. Determine how many people you're arranging transportation for and book the vehicle accordingly. Sometimes this is simply a thoughtful way to keep your guests from worrying, and other times it's the only option for getting them to the wedding. If it's the latter, you'll need a system for ensuring guests board the right vehicle at the right place. Enlist some responsible friends to be captains and check people off a list. If guests are missing, these friends can try tracking them down—they may be at the wrong pick-up spot!

If the ride is long enough, this is another opportunity for fun and personalization. You can add an extra touch by playing special music and providing a beverage. In advance, always make sure the drivers or transportation companies have explicit directions for the number of guests, the destination, and the route.

JMK TIP

Don't forget the children! If you're organizing any transportation for little kids, it's imperative to ask about car seats. You don't want your sister-in-law to miss your wedding because her child doesn't have a ride.

PARKING

As a Manhattanite, I don't often think about parking while heading somewhere, but it's important to consider in most places other than metropolitan cities. Does your venue have ample parking for the number of cars expected? Will guests park their own cars, or will there be a valet? Do you want to cover the cost of parking or have your guests pay for themselves? Confirm these details in advance to avoid any day-of headaches. If the event will take place somewhere without readily available rideshares or taxis, have a plan in place for any guests who overdo it at the open bar and can't drive.

WEATHER

One thing you certainly can't control during your wedding week is the weather. Ideally, if any part of your event is meant to be outdoors, you know what the contingency plan is. Some of this depends on where your wedding will be and how consistent or predictable the weather is. A few days before the event, you'll need to make a final call on decisions such as installing a rain tent, adding heat, or providing additional shade coverage. Even if the whole event will be indoors, confirm whether your venue has a coat check area available and whether you need to notify them in advance for it to be staffed. Can you get from the car to the entrance without getting wet? If not, a thoughtful touch is having attendants with large umbrellas greet guests and escort them in as they pull up. What about an

OPENING NIGHT

outdoor wedding with extreme heat? Is there an area with umbrellas or shade available? If it will be very cold, will there be heaters or blankets? What if a storm passes right before the event? Even if the sky is clear, make sure the grounds are suitable for walking. No one wants their Manolo Blahniks digging into the mud.

JMK TIP

When creating your plan B, don't forget about photo locations. If you've planned for your pre-event photos to be taken outdoors but it might rain, consult your photographer in advance to arrange where they'll take place.

GIFTS

Many couples like to show thanks to anyone who was closely involved in helping, such as wedding party members. Sometimes these gifts can be practical, such as what all of you might wear while getting ready or an accessory that becomes part of the wedding look. If you'd like to do something like this, know that the earlier you get this out of the way, the better. You don't want to be scrambling for these gifts or filling out cards the day before.

Many couples also like to give something to one another on the day of. I do find this moment to be one of the most tender to witness, but you also might feel like you've spent everything you have on the wedding. If that's the case, express how you feel in a card or a note. This is your day to savor with one another!

FINAL PAYMENTS & GRATUITIES

You'll likely have some balances due the day of the wedding, so be sure to prepare for this. You should know in advance whether the venue plans to make a large charge, so make sure the funds are available in your account or your credit card company is aware. You don't want a catering manager calling you during wedding portraits to say they can't serve your guests until the funds clear.

We live in a society where workers are reliant on their tips in addition to their wages, so you'll also want to determine who from your vendor list is in that category and prepare. Review the list of everyone who'll be working, from bathroom attendants to valets. Some JMK clients tip only servers, bartenders, and musicians, while others tip every single person who works on the day of. This is up to you, but again, plan for this in advance, not only in your budgeting but in how you plan to distribute money. See whether a gratuity is already included in what you're paying for or you'll need to tip that night. Some vendors add this to your bill, some handle this digitally through apps like Venmo, and some require cash. For any teams you plan to tip, ask your point of contact just how many there will be and what is standard. If you'll be handing out cash, place everything into labeled envelopes in advance and give them to someone you trust who'll be responsible for distributing them. This is an excellent job for someone who wants to help but might be less involved, like a dad!

HONEYMOON

Even if you've used every tool in this book and had an entirely stress-free experience, there's nothing like being able to celebrate more afterward alone and somewhere fabulous. The finances of a honeymoon are different for everyone. Some couples pay for it themselves in entirety, while others get contributions from their parents. It's common now to register for items you'll use on your honeymoon. Since your budget has everything to do with this, you should make preliminary decisions about a honeymoon right at the beginning of the wedding planning process.

You don't have to take a honeymoon immediately after your wedding. For a variety of reasons, it has become increasingly popular to travel later. It might be easier for you to spread out the time

OPENING NIGHT

you need off from work, and planning a trip and wedding at the same time might be too much. You may also have out-of-town guests you want to spend more time with before they leave, and if you're not going away, you can consider a brief "minimoon" before returning to reality.

If you're planning a honeymoon yourselves, identify what kind of experience interests the two of you and spend your money on something that supports your ideals and lifestyles. If you plan to leave right after the wedding, pack beforehand. You don't want this task to be waiting for you the morning after you said your I dos.

PACK-UP

We discussed starting your shopping list as you prepare your wardrobe and toiletries, but you also need to consider the outgoing part of this process. Once you've reached the end and had your last dance, the last thing you'll want is to make a ton of decisions or be worried. If flowers are left, do you want your guests to take them, or do they need to be transported somewhere? What about the gifts people brought? Who'll be holding the marriage license you signed that needs to get mailed? Are you taking the top tier of your wedding cake? What about extra programs, menus, cocktail napkins, and personalized escort cards? If you changed into a second look, who's responsible for taking your first outfit? Take some pressure off yourselves by assigning members of your wedding party and/or your siblings to take care of these responsibilities. If one collects your cards, another the cake, and so on, you can relax knowing no wedding item will be left behind!

RUN OF SHOW

In the workbook, there's a document I've mentioned a few times called Run of Show, and this part of the process is now paramount. We originally used it to establish the main blocks of time, such as when your ceremony and reception will start. Now you need to elaborate with the minute-to-minute schedule that you and everyone working on your wedding should follow. You identified hard facts, such as when cocktail hour is; decided what wedding moments, traditions, or new creations you wanted to execute; and confirmed potential ideas, such as a best friend's toast and whether a drag queen will be popping out of your wedding cake. With these details solidified, you can now use this sheet to work backward and document final logistics for the run of your show, such as when the drag queen must arrive, wait, get into drag, and be preset into the cake for it to be presented on time.

When constructing your Run of Show, do so with anyone who needs to weigh in, including the caterer and musicians. Pay attention to details such as how long the food service will take and when your band might need a break. Review the order of events for everything that will be happening, and create the Run of Show with all the details. Spend time with this, really thinking about how one moment flows into the next. Orchestrate movement throughout, spread out activities such as toasts and special dances, and interweave everything with what's being served. Caterers might tell you what they like to do versus what they have to do, but remember: *You* are the designer. Make it beautiful. Make it special. Make it your own! Finalizing the Run of Show is the step that should allow you to truly feel ready to open.

In the workbook, I provide several examples of a Run of Show, from simpler weddings to the most elaborate, and here's just one of them:

OPENING NIGHT

SATURDAY

9:15 AM	Friend Picks Up Getting Ready Food Order
10:30 AM	Hair & Makeup Arrival & Setup in West Room (3rd floor) Getting Ready Food Arrival Onsite
11:00 AM	Hair & Makeup Begins Photography Begins with Detail Shots & Getting Ready Brides in Hair & Makeup Florist Loads In Cake Delivery
12:00 PM	Bridal Hair & Makeup Complete Brides Get Dressed
12:30 PM	Brides Escorted to First Look AV Equipment Load In
1:00 PM	First Look Suburban Limo Arrives
1:30 PM	Brides and Photo Team Depart for Portraits Around the City
2:30 PM	Wedding Party Meets Brides in Park for Group Shots
3:30 PM	All Return from Photoshoot Hair & Makeup Touch Ups Hair & Makeup Concludes Ceremony Area Photo Ready
4:00 PM	Family Photos Sound Crew Load In
5:00 PM	Musicians Arrives Step & Repeat Set Programs Pre Set

CONTINUED →

WE DO

SATURDAY

RUN OF SHOW	**5:30 PM**	Wedding Party/Family Photos Complete Marriage License Pre-Sign Ceremony Musicians Begin Prelude
	6:00 PM	Invite Passed Champagne Offered to Guests
	6:30 PM	Ceremony Start Time
	7:00 PM	Cocktail Hour Begins Time Alone for Brides Passed Canapes & Specialty Cocktails Jazz Trio Plays Step & Repeat Relocated to Photobooth
	7:15 PM	Brides Join Cocktail Hour
	7:22 PM	Sunset
	7:50 PM	Brides Preview of the Dining Room
	8:00 PM	Reception Begins Guests Find Their Seats Wine Poured Orders Taken
	8:15 PM	Intro of Wedding Party Intro of Brides into First Dance Into Opening Dance Set
	8:40 PM	First Course Welcome Toast from All Four Parents
	9:00 PM	First Course Cleared

CONTINUED →

OPENING NIGHT

SATURDAY	
9:15 PM	Main Course Served
9:40 PM	Toasts by Best Women Joint Fathers/Daughters Dance
9:50 PM	Into Next Dance Set
10:00 PM	Brides Change into Second Look
10:25 PM	Brides Reenter
10:30 PM	Cake Cutting/Coffee Served Toast by Grooms
10:45 PM	Drag Queen Performance
11:00 PM	Final Dance Set Til the End Passed Espresso Martini Shots Pass Fiber Optic Wands
11:30 PM	Passed Late Night Bites
11:40 PM	Night Street Shots with Brides
11:45 PM	Arrival of After Party Buses
11:55 PM	Announcement of Last Dance
12:00 AM	Reception Ends Guests Board Busses for After Party All Gifts & Pack Out Items Taken to Brides' Room Floral, Lighting & AV Load Out

Your Run of Show serves as the most important document that all vendors will work from. Earlier on, you decided whether you needed to hire an event planner or someone to just run the event the day of, or maybe your venue or caterer has provided someone. Regardless, someone needs to be in charge of running the show, and it cannot be you. Be sure to discuss at length with this person or these people all the points on your Run of Show until you feel confident that they understand all the moving pieces you've organized. While this document should include everything and everyone related to your event, it does not need to be seen by your guests. Frankly, showing a friend when lighting is being installed might lead to unwanted criticism.

For family and friends who've scheduled tasks beyond simply showing up to the wedding, I recommend creating a shortened version of this list that includes things like hair and makeup needs, transportation arrangements, and family photo call time. Put down only what additional times and locations they need to know!

CURTAIN UP

You made it! It's the day of the show, y'all! Your custom-designed event is finally here; opening night has arrived! You're now a calm, cool, and excited couple who'll be enjoying the festivities, comforted by all the organizational tools you used to prepare to say, "WE DO!" Our time planning together might be concluding, but everything you've worked toward on this journey is finally here.

My final words to you are these: No matter how meticulously you organize this event, chances are something might happen that isn't part of the plan. Sometimes things are delivered incorrectly, someone misses a cue, or the weather apps are just completely wrong. Whatever the case may be, the most important thing now is to let go of trying to control what you can't. Be as present as possible for the experience, and understand that even if something completely unexpected happens, you still get to marry one another.

CURTAIN CALL

Congratulations! You did it! Chances are the next morning will feel quite surreal. Remember to enjoy this feeling. You accomplished not only planning a wedding but officially marrying each other. Celebrate the love you have for each other today and every day for the rest of your lives.

Hopefully you had the time of your life at your wedding, but be prepared for some post-wedding blues. They're common after all the excitement and anticipation you grew accustomed to fade away. But you got to wed your chosen partner, and isn't that the most exciting part of it all? Whether you're leaving for a honeymoon or just resuming life as a wedded couple, allow yourself some time to indulge and enjoy everything you just accomplished. You deserve it, and it's time to live your lives as a wedded couple.

As I say to all JMK couples, planning a wedding and living in a marriage are two totally different concepts. When in doubt, remember those feelings you had when you exchanged vows, felt all the love from your family and friends, and woke up the next day knowing the two of you pulled off what dreams are made of. You created a show that told your love story, and now you get to live in and enjoy what will hopefully be a very long run!

APPENDIX: EXPERT INSIGHTS

I've worked on hundreds of wedding ceremonies and love collaborating with couples to make their events truly unique. I've also been fascinated by some of the religious officiants we've hired who specialize in nontraditional weddings. Since religion can play such a big role in a wedding ceremony, I wanted to dive a bit deeper with scholars of Christianity, Judaism, and Islam, so I reached out to several experts.

First I chatted with author, activist, and public theologian Brandan Robertson, an openly gay ordained minister in the United Church of Christ and pastor of Sunnyside Reformed Church in NYC. He works at the intersection of spirituality, sexuality, and social renewal. I asked him how he interprets the rules of a wedding, and here are his insights:

> Queer couples have interesting considerations. A lot of them have taken on the heterosexual and religious idea that marriage needs to be a lifelong commitment, but many also feel that's unreasonable or unrealistic.

So, I work with couples to think through what they are actually committing to. My religion teaches it is covenant, which is a commitment between two people and their higher power to something. Many of the weddings I've performed had couples who didn't commit to a lifelong covenant but to the season of it, and I restructured the marriage they were entering to be something that actually worked for them. In these ceremonies, we still reclaim our scriptures and reinterpret stories from the Bible, such as David and Goliath and Ruth and Naomi. It's more beautiful to witness an honest commitment than one that isn't reflective of what the couple wants.

When I work with couples, we begin by looking at the Anglican and Lutheran traditional prayer books and the orders that are listed in them. Then we deconstruct what's suggested. There's no actual script for a marriage ceremony in scripture. We use resources that have been established in the past fifty years from progressive pastors and churches. The Bible does not state that marriage is between a man and a woman. It contains stories that include polygamy and people who have concubines. It's not a very pro-marriage book, and that's a good thing, as it promotes honesty within a marriage. No one should feel they have to abandon their religion or faith to live authentically.

Next I chatted with Rabbi Matt Green, who leads Congregation Beth Elohim and is also gay. As the director of Brooklyn Jews, he guides the synagogue's young community of Brooklynites who are seeking connection to Jewish culture. I asked him how he plans for a wedding between a man and a woman versus between two men or two women in a Jewish ceremony, and these were his insights:

> There are four components to consider for couples who are not heteronormative:

APPENDIX: EXPERT INSIGHTS

1. The **ketubah** requires [specific] Hebrew language about the couple, which is gendered and typically states a groom is acquiring a bride. The ketubah is an opportunity for an untraditional couple to play with the language.
2. **Erusim** is the first section in a Jewish wedding ceremony and is a prayer of betrothal. This traditional orthodox blessing is about separating out your partner from having forbidden sexual relationships [but] permits you to have sex with your partner. This is rarely appropriate for any modern couple, and the reform movement and progressive rabbis have offered new blessings instead. It's another opportunity for the couple to define these terms [for themselves]. It wouldn't be appropriate for a couple who doesn't plan to be monogamous. In some cases, couples have worked to establish this section as a declaration to be accepting and honest with one another.
3. The **vows** in a Jewish traditional ceremony typically have a groom recite something very specific that translates to, "Behold, you are now my object." For an untraditional couple, this is another place to modify the language or write their own vows all together.
4. The **Sheva Brachot**, or seven blessings, ends with two blessings thanking God, who gladdens the bride and groom. For couples who don't use those titles, we get creative with the language. And more expansive than that, couples can also come up with new seven blessings. Also, the traditional way of doing this was for the bride to circle the groom seven times. With nontraditional couples, I encourage them to each do three and one together.

I then asked, "When I'm organizing Jewish heteronormative ceremonies versus not, we pay close attention to how the parents escort the bride down the aisle and what side the bride and groom are standing on, which is opposite of how it's typically done in Christian weddings. Is there somewhere in Jewish law that defines this?

> There is not. In Jewish law, there's a category known as "minhag," which means "custom." Customs can be powerful but are not law. For instance, wearing a yarmulke is custom but not law. Customs change from place to place. Only Ashkenazi ceremonies have the seven blessings and not Sephardic ones. So, there are no rules about the processional order, sides, or who stands underneath a chuppah. It's a Western tradition for a bride to be handed off by her father.
>
> Probably one of the most recognizable customs that concludes a Jewish ceremony is the breaking of the glass. When I started doing same-sex weddings, I would always ask the couple if they wanted to break two, and here is where LGBTQ+ weddings really started to influence all weddings. Now I ask every couple, and many modern straight brides choose to also break a glass.

Finally, I discussed ceremonies with Dr. Mike Mohamed Ghouse, founder and president of the Center for Pluralism and the director of the World Muslim Congress. I mentioned that many people feel any type of religious wedding is not for an LGBTQ+ couple and asked him how he approaches working with a nontraditional couple:

> The wedding is a union between two individuals. While the Quran does not prohibit such unions, cultural traditions often do. Historically, many religions and movements faced severe persecution in the beginning, leading them to seek preservation through procreation and protecting their communities. This has resulted in the development of protectionist attitudes toward LGBTQ+ marriages.

> However, that motivation no longer exists today, and the LGBTQ+ community is an integral part of the world. No single religion is followed by the entire population, nor will the LGBTQ+ community be followed by the entire population. We must learn to respect and accept the otherness of others.
>
> Whether the couple is traditional or nontraditional, they are two souls seeking harmony with each other. We make no distinctions in our approach; it remains the same for every couple.

This led me to ask, "What changes do you make when working with LGBTQ+ couples versus heterosexual couples?"

> The primary change involves language. Some LGBTQ+ couples prefer to refer to each other as "spouses," "husband and wife," or "partners," while others may choose "bride and groom." Our focus is on the union of two souls rather than the specific language or steps involved in the ceremony. Every wedding will be customized to suit the wants and needs of the couple, with a touch of religion or religions in case of interfaith marriages.

What aspects of Muslim traditions can LGBTQ+ couples personalize for their weddings?

> It begins with the couple's intention to unite as one (*niyya*). Traditional verses from the Quran will still be recited as they are with all couples. Personalization comes through the couple's unique language, individuality, and involvement of their families.

I asked whether there are any customs of a Muslim wedding that cannot be performed for an LGBTQ+ couple, and he said, "No. We treat all couples the same, and no kissing in public."

We wrapped our discussion with me asking whether he has any advice for an LGBTQ+ couple who wishes to marry within the Muslim faith, and his answer was impactful:

> When people meet in college, the workplace, at family gatherings, or online, they may find mutual attraction and compatibility. My advice is to simply live your life without feeling the need to flaunt your identity as a gay couple. It ultimately does not matter to others—it's your life. True peace of mind comes from accepting each person's uniqueness as a gift from God and respecting their religion, culture, race, ethnicity, and way of life without prejudice.

As someone who regularly plans weddings for nontraditional couples, I know that incorporating religious elements can often be challenging, fraught with triggers and trauma, or incredibly modified and beautiful. Anything you feel authentically connected to or is of importance to you should find a way into your wedding.

ACKNOWLEDGMENTS

The year that I wrote this, I spent a tremendous amount of time reflecting on my life. I often look around and think that as a child I never dreamed big enough to have all this. I am incredibly grateful for the following people.

First and foremost, thank you to Jenn Grace, Alexander Loutsenko, Nelly Murario, Emily Ribeiro and the entire team at Publish Your Purpose for making this book possible. Your guidance has made this process enriching and enjoyable. And to my editor Nancy Graham-Tillman, you truly knocked it out of the park. You listened, understood, and heard my voice and made it play to the back of the house.

Thank you to Dr. Mike Ghouse, theologian Brandan Robertson, and Rabbi Matt Green, not only for your insights in the book but for working with couples around the world who've benefited from your guidance on the intersection of religion and the nontraditional.

As stated in my intro, I've learned something from every wedding I've ever been a part of. Thank you to all the couples who've trusted me over the years to be a part of your planning journey. My reputation in the business is that I always get the best clients, and it's absolutely true!

To my industry colleagues, I cannot thank you enough! It's one thing to be appreciative that I work in a celebratory field, and it's another to feel so constantly inspired by all of you. Other planners who could've been competition instead became dear friends. Everyone I've gotten to collaborate with in some way, from designers, chefs, and musical geniuses to people who work coat checks and operate the sanitation station, is an important part of what we execute. I'm grateful for your ideas and work and that we have fun while doing it.

I would be nothing without the "Co." in my business's name. Thank you to every single one of you who has worked as a part of team JMK, including every freelancer who has understood the assignment and been an extension of the brand. Jason Michael Snow, whether you're serving on-site, creating music for our couples, or determining whether my jokes in the book land, you're always a dream. Peter Porte, I will forever be grateful for your invaluable time and insights the year I went out on my own. To Alex Paige, Giovanni Bonaventura, Michael Hartung, Luke Hamilton, Christina Jackson, and Kasey Graham, I never could've pulled off everything without you, and you're all such lovely humans on top of being excellent at the work. And to the one and only Dani Spieler, thank you for adding "best work wife in the world" to your multi-hyphenation. There would be no Co. without you.

So much of my career has been made possible by everyone who rallied, fought, educated, fundraised, and legislated so that fellow members of the LGBTQ+ community could marry. Thank you to each and every one of you, and please know I will always continue to fight alongside you in whatever challenges our community continues to face.

And just like that, I'm at the part where I need to thank some friends. There are so many of you who I just adore, and I would not be where or who I am today without you. In no way can this be a conclusive list of all the wonderful humans I consider family, but Mitch just wants to say thank you for the years of laughs, tears, hugs, and nicknames to Erin DePaula, Molly Tynes, Jove Meyer, Kyle Torrence,

ACKNOWLEDGMENTS

Lora Lee Gayer, Eric Jaffe, Alysha Umphress, Cody Williams, Kate Bond, Craig Gates, Ben Baur, Matt Medaglia, Ian Weiss, Mike Robotti, Joel Bauer, Chase Thompson, Eric Stroud, Allison Yacker, Courtney Gazaleh, Christopher Orne, Jason Esposito, Jason Harder, Wendell Odom, Ben Sands and Tino DeMartino. I look forward to future memories in Barnaby's Ballroom and beyond!

Thank you to the Mount Pleasant Animal Shelter, where I rescued my best friend Barnaby. He can't read this, but every day he shows me he's grateful with his signature underbite and side-eye.

And to the most incredible family, thank you for being you! It's so special to have such a network of aunts, uncles, and cousins who all not only love me and support my career but have been so welcoming and accepting to those of us who identify as LGBTQ+. Marni and Casey, can you believe it all started with your wedding? I'm grateful for that, in addition to all the love and sass you give me every day. And look what we did! Emerson and Tucker, you truly are the light of my lives, and being Uncle Jay is my favorite role of all in life. And none of this would be possible without the iconic Genie and Jeff. Thank you for being, well, simply the best!

ABOUT THE AUTHOR

Jason Mitchell Kahn is the owner and creative director of Jason Mitchell Kahn & Co., a boutique agency that specializes in planning and executing events for nontraditional couples. His work has been featured in *Vogue*, *The New York Times*, and *People*; he's been listed as one of the Best Wedding Planners of the Year in *Brides* magazine; and he's hailed as "Broadway's Wedding Planner" by *Playbill*. He's also a highly sought-after  speaker on inclusivity in weddings and is the author of *Getting Groomed*, the first wedding planner published for gay grooms.

Jason served as Director of Weddings and Editorial for *Men's Vows* magazine, and before launching Jason Mitchell Kahn & Co., he served as the resident wedding planner for Shiraz Events, overseeing the company's market in New York, Los Angeles, and London. Prior to that, he worked for several years at Soho House New York as the event and banquet manager and quickly became known as "the in-house wedding expert." There he worked with couples on planning their special day in addition to doing freelance wedding planning.

While weddings are Jason's favorite type of event, at Soho House he also designed, planned, and ran fashion shows, book launches, art festivals, movie premieres, opening nights, gala dinners, and post-parties after award shows. The job took him around the world, from Oscar parties in Los Angeles to events held in chateaus in Cannes, and even an underground subway station in Toronto.

Jason brings to weddings his passion for drama honed from his career and education in theater. He attended the conservatory New World School of the Arts and graduated magna cum laude with a B.F.A. in Theatre from the University of Florida. Two of his plays, *The Boys Upstairs* and *The Red Box*, had professional premieres in New York and have since had productions around the world. Jason approaches all weddings with his playwriting background: What is the couple's version of their most beautiful story to be told?

He lives on the upper-west side of Manhattan with his terrier Barnaby.

www.ingramcontent.com/pod-product-compliance
Lightning Source LLC
Chambersburg PA
CBHW041310240426
43661CB00064B/2883